Fight the Powers
What the Bible Says About the Relationship Between Spiritual Forces and Human Governments

CODY COOK

2018
Cantus Firmus Media

Some sections of this work include modified transcripts of podcasts and essays previously released at www.cantus-firmus.com, small selections from my book *A Second Adam*, and excerpts from an essay I wrote for www.rethinkinghell.com. The latter was used with permission.

Cover image designed by Jackson Ferrell. To see more of Jackson's work, visit http://www.bigjstudios.com/

Seven headed dragon illustration at chapter headings and back cover from a 13th century British and French illuminated manuscript of Revelation housed in the Morgan Library & Museum. Pierpont Morgan Library. MS M.524.

ISBN: 9781717880031

Thanks to
Ben Highley, Scott Johnson, and Michael Schellman for reading early portions of this work and offering suggestions for improvement.

A very special thanks to
My wife Raven for her support and patience while I did research and writing for this book. I love you, dear heart.

TABLE OF CONTENTS

Foreword

We Americans find ourselves at a precarious time in our nation's history. We are a severely fractured nation, the likes of which we have seen only two times. The years leading to the Civil War and the period of Vietnam were perhaps the most tumultuous times in our nation – until now. It seems that everyone is screaming against something or someone. Violence is on the rise. People are looking for safety and security. People are looking to the state for answers. Some in the church seek the state for protection and safety.

As a Christian, I like to think we are the most discerning people on the planet. Yet, I am amazed at how quickly we can get caught up in politics and kingdoms that we have no part in. Make no mistake, I am equally guilty. How quickly we forget that we are immigrants here on earth, "longing for a better country – a heavenly one," as the writer of Hebrews remarks on the forefathers of our faith. Through the writer of the epistle of Hebrews, the Holy Spirit reminds us of something Jesus constantly taught: we are not of this world.

The role of the church in relation to the state under which she finds herself is always relevant. Why is that? Because of how easily we are caught up, just like anyone else, in the currents of nationalism, patriotism, and public opinion. If anything, right now in America, Christ's followers should be among the first to raise an eyebrow as the world asks, "what's going on here?"

Scripture has answered that since the beginning. How quickly we forget that we were born into a war zone. Eden's ashes smolder as humanity sings Lamech's murderous song all the way to the top of Babel. Murder, violence, and blind nationalism continually poison the water and all humans, even God's people, are seduced by the allure of political power and social status.

What is God's answer? We are in a spiritual war. Empire versus the Kingdom of God. One wields the sword of violence, the other the Sword of the Spirit. One coerces through violence, the other humbles herself to service. The two are at odds, and the world systems align not with God, but Babylon. The role of the demonic and political systems is explained from Genesis to Revelation.

I met Cody at his invitation to appear on his podcast. Meeting him for the first time, I can say it felt like finding a long-lost friend. He is humble, kind, and seeks God in all things. I value his insight and exegetical research. He is a thoughtful, kind Christian man, and I am blessed to know him.

In the pages that follow, Cody weaves a masterful study. He is not here to convince you of his opinion or recruit you to his camp. He poses difficult questions, yes, but he doesn't force his view on you. He simply puts forth the biblical narrative and leads you from beginning to end to bring you to the place where you draw your own conclusions.

His biblical approach is not a journey in proof-texting, as are many on this subject. His consideration of the entire biblical narrative brings proper context, not popular opinion. His use of early church sources and modern-day interpretations are timely and succinct.

If you seek truth, you will find great rewards in this great work. The relationship between the Church and State will always be a battle. How we respond considering God's word will decide where we stand when the kingdoms of the earth fade away. Let us be defined as "peacemakers," that we will build the Kingdom together, regardless of the evil set against us. Let us be a voice of reason in chaos. Let us follow the resurrected Lord Jesus to a better country. After all, we're simply passing through this one.

Christus Victor,
Scott C. Johnson

Scott Johnson is a demonologist, exorcist, and the senior minister at Crosspointe Church of Christ in Franklin, Ohio. You can find him at www.turningovertables.com.

FIGHT THE POWERS

Introduction

Biblical Christianity has always understood that the demonic realm exists and that it impacts the physical realm. In American evangelical Christianity, there has even been acceptance of the idea that Satan was in some sense behind the scenes of particularly authoritarian and despicable governments like Hitler's Third Reich or Stalin's Russia. But the scriptures go much further on the subject of the demonic and the state than to merely target the occasional despot as demonically influenced.

What is the state? Is it a divinely ordained tool for justice? A weapon in the hands of demonic forces? Both?

For many American evangelicals, it is taken as a given that state policy is to be crafted with the mindset that America was and is meant to be a Christian nation, chosen by God to do great things.

In contrast, the Christian scriptures seem to present a different vision of the state—a vision where the state is at this present time under the influence of hostile spiritual forces which make a complete union of church and nation both impossible and immoral. But if this is so, how should Christians relate to political power? Would it be appropriate to vote, to lobby for policy, or to serve in the military?

In the following pages, I hope to outline biblical data which posits a close connection between political and demonic[1] power.

---

1   Scholars debate over the technical application of the New Testament term

For those who take scripture seriously, these data should provide a foundation for the models we develop of church and state relations, which is the subject of the second part of this present volume.[2] For those who don't, I hope you will nevertheless be intrigued by this fascinating, though often ignored, picture of power as presented in scripture.

It has been my goal in the writing and revising of this book to follow the advice of my Old Testament professor Dr. Phillip Brown: "Make sure you are clear in your distinction between explicit, implicit, and potential conclusions, and provide justification for all assertions." This is particularly important for a topic such as this one due to its controversial nature and implications for Christian practice. I hope I have followed his advice conscientiously. Though my conclusion—that a thoroughgoing relationship between church and state is compromised by the spiritual nature of political power—may be somewhat controversial, it is my hope that the care with which I have handled scripture will bear it out to those who are serious about hearing and obeying the word of God.

---

demon (whether it should be applied only to fallen angels, the disembodied sons of the Nephilim, etc.). An overview of some of these views can be found in chapter IV: The Reality and Identity of Demons in Unger's *Biblical Demonology: A Study of Spiritual Forces at Work Today*. I am using the word to refer generally to angelic powers which are under the judgment of God.

2   I include in the group of those taking scripture seriously even those with a more flexible view of infallibility. Even religiously liberal Christians who deny to some extent the existence of the demonic should still want to grapple with the practical application of the biblical idea of a demonic influence on the political realm, whatever they interpret that to mean.

PART 1

The Powers According to Scripture

FIGHT THE POWERS

CODY COOK

And though this world, with devils filled, should threaten to undo us,
We will not fear, for God hath willed His truth to triumph through us;
The Prince of Darkness grim, we tremble not for him;
His rage we can endure, for lo, his doom is sure,
One little word shall fell him.

That word above all earthly pow'rs, no thanks to them, abideth;
The Spirit and the gifts are ours through Him Who with us sideth;
Let goods and kindred go, this mortal life also;
The body they may kill: God's truth abideth still,
His kingdom is forever.

-Martin Luther
"A Mighty Fortress Is Our God"

FIGHT THE POWERS

1
The Old Testament

A biblical theology of the intersection between demonic and political power must begin in the Old Testament. What follows is an examination of the most relevant passages for constructing such a theology.

Genesis

Genesis 1:26-28 presents us with a picture of humanity which has dominion over the world even as it functions under the direct authority of God:

"Then God said, 'Let us make [humanity] in our image, after our likeness. And let them have dominion over the fish of the sea and over the birds of the heavens and over the livestock and over all the earth and over every creeping thing that creeps on the earth . . . Be fruitful and multiply and fill the earth and subdue it, and have dominion over the fish of the sea and over the birds of the heavens and over every living thing that moves on the earth'" (ESV).

Old Testament scholar Eugene Merrill mused of this passage: "What is lacking apparently after the whole cosmos has been spoken into existence is its management, a caretaker as it were who will govern it all according to the will of the Creator. He could have done it himself without mediation, but for reasons never revealed in the sacred record, God elected to reign through a subordinate, a surrogate king responsible only to him."[3]

John Walton, reflecting along similar lines, noted that:
"The image of God as an Old Testament concept... pertains to the role and function that God has given humanity (found, for example, in 'subdue;' and 'rule,' Gen 1:28), to the identity that he has bequeathed on us (i.e., it is, by definition, who we are as human beings), and to the way that we serve as his substitute by representing his presence in the world. When Assyrian kings made images of themselves to be placed in conquered cities or at important borders, they were communicating that they were, in effect, continually present in that place."[4]

In a sense, this is what society is meant to be—the ethical administration of and care for world resources. However, the Genesis account presents this ideal as having been corrupted as the result of human sin. The intended dominion of man over the world and under God is subverted in the creation account by a shadowy figure known as the serpent. In later times the serpent is explicitly identified with Satan, a figure whom is described in the New Testament as the god and prince of this world (2 Corinthians 4:4, John 12:31), which suggests that Satan not only undermined man's dominion in the garden, but also usurped it. As biblical scholar and demonologist Merrill Unger wrote:
"These [the earthly kingdoms] were not delivered unto the devil by God. They had been delivered unto him by man. Man had yielded to him, and consequently these kingdoms had all passed under the mastery of the devil."[5]

The next time that man's dominion over the earth is discussed in Genesis is in chapter 11—the tower of Babel account. At Babel,

---

3   Eugene H. Merrill, Everlasting Dominion, Broadman & Holman, 2006, Kindle edition
4   John H. Walton, The Lost World of Adam and Eve: Genesis 2-3 and the Human Origins Debate, IVP Academic, 2015, Kindle edition.
5   Merrill F. Unger, Biblical Demonology, Kregel, 1994, Kindle edition.

man sought to exercise dominion over the world by organizing under one government to build a tower which reaches the heavens so that they might "make a name" for themselves.

Instead of God cheering man on for taking the initiative to restore his dominion, He expresses concern over what fallen mankind might be capable of if unified under one political authority. The account tells us that God then confused their language so that they would have no other choice but to separate from one another into various groups. Later Jewish thinkers identified these various groups as the seventy nations detailed in Genesis chapter 10.

Deuteronomy

Keeping in mind what we read in Genesis—that Satan usurped man's authority over the earth and God separated mankind into various nations to prevent the great dangers of centralized human power—we can better understand a strange (to our western minds) passage in Deuteronomy 32. In this chapter, Moses recounts to Israel what God had done for them. He encourages his listeners to ask their fathers about "the days of old," the:

"years of many generations . . . when the Most High gave to the nations their inheritance, when he divided mankind, [and] he fixed the borders of the peoples according to the number of the sons of God. But the Lord's portion is his people, Jacob his allotted heritage."[6]

---

6   Deuteronomy 32:7-9, ESV. There is an important textual variant here. The ESV and some other more modern translations follow an ancient reading from the Dead Sea Scrolls of "sons of God." This is similar to the Greek Septuagint's "ἀγγέλων θεοῦ" (angels of God) while the Masoretic text (and many older English translations) reads "בְּנֵי יִשְׂרָאֵל" (sons of Israel). G.F. Moore (as cited in Russell, p. 248) points out that even the Masoretic could point, though more obliquely, to the same meaning since Exodus 1:5 likewise gives the number of the children of Israel as seventy—the same number in the table of nations in Genesis 10. In any case, the Masoretic reading does not point as explicitly to the notion of angels over nations as the Septuagint does. It seems to the author that the original reading is "sons

13

In Old Testament usage, the term "sons of God" refers to angelic beings.[7] In other words, Deuteronomy 32:8-9 seems to be communicating that God has placed lesser spiritual powers over the nations but chose Israel as His special people.

D. S. Russell, who also contended that all of the intertestamental literature which writes of spiritual powers over nations goes back to this passage, understood it as:
"describ[ing] the division of the nations of mankind and the choosing of Israel to be God's own people. . . All the nations of the earth are given over into the control of angelic powers, but Israel is reserved for Yahweh alone."[8]

Biblical scholar and Semitic languages expert Michael Heiser concurs:
"Deuteronomy 32:8–9 describes how Yahweh's dispersal of the nations at Babel resulted in his disinheriting those nations as his people . . . The statement in Deuteronomy 32:9 that 'the LORD's [i.e., Yahweh's] portion is his people, Jacob his allotted heritage' tips us off that a contrast in affection and ownership is intended. Yahweh in effect decided that the people of the world's nations were no longer going to be in relationship to him. He would begin anew. He would enter into covenant relationship

---

of God" since it better explains the revisions "sons of Israel" and "angels of God," which appear to be emendations from embarrassment. The later Palestinian Targum combines at least two of these variant readings in an interesting way:
"He cast the lot among the seventy angels, the princes of the nations with whom is the revelation to oversee the city, even at that time He established the limits of the nations according to the sum of the number of the seventy souls of Israel who went down into Mizraim [Egypt]"
(https://juchre.org/targums/comp/deut32.htm).

7   See Job 1:6, Job 38:7, Genesis 6:2, and Psalm 82:6
8   D. S. Russell, The Method and Message of Jewish Apocalyptic, The Westminster Press, 1964. Clinton Arnold quotes these words from Russell approvingly in his *Powers of Darkness: Principalities & Powers in Paul's Letters* (Intervarsity Press, 1992)

14

CODY COOK

with a new people that did not yet exist: Israel."[9]

The chapter goes on to speak about God's authority to judge both Israel and the nations—even those nations whom God's angels had been given authority over—so this notion is not a challenge to God's sovereignty.[10]

We can establish, then, a train of thought on this matter in the first five books of the Bible traditionally attributed to Moses:

1. God makes mankind to rule over the earth under His direct authority.
2. Satan subverts that rule.
3. God divides humanity into nations to prevent them from becoming too powerful and thus dangerous.
4. God assigns angelic beings authority over these nations and chooses Israel as His special people.

What becomes clear in other Old Testament writings is that these angelic beings do not perform their duties admirably but oppose God and His people by their malevolent influence over the nations in their charge.

Psalms

Psalm 82 gives us a unique look into the heavenly realm, pulling back the curtain so that we may see the powers behind the powers. Asaph the psalmist describes the scene. It is one of judgment, namely God's judgment upon corrupted powers in the scene of a heavenly council:

God has taken his place in the divine council;
in the midst of the gods he holds judgment:
"How long will you judge unjustly
and show partiality to the wicked?

---

9 Michael S. Heiser, The Unseen Realm: Recovering the Supernatural Worldview of the Bible, Lexham Press, 2015, Kindle edition.
10 See verses 39-43.

15

FIGHT THE POWERS

. . . Give justice to the weak and the fatherless;
maintain the right of the afflicted and the destitute.
Rescue the weak and the needy;
deliver them from the hand of the wicked..."

I said, "You are gods,
sons of the Most High, all of you;
nevertheless, like men you shall die,
and fall like any prince."
Arise, O God, judge the earth;
for you shall inherit all the nations!
-Psalm 82, ESV

In the western Christian tradition this passage has traditionally been viewed by exegetes as referring to God condemning human leaders and judges for perverting justice. John Wesley, in his explanatory notes on this Psalm, argues that "judges and magistrates are called gods, because they have their commission from God, and act as his deputies." When the Most High God tells these "gods" that they will die like men, Wesley reasons that he only means "like ordinary men," though is silent on the verse's parallel statement, "and fall like any prince," which suggests he is contrasting them with human princes.[11]

On the other end of the Calvinist/Arminian divide, Charles Spurgeon likewise takes the view that human magistrates are the focus on this Psalm, arguing:
"They are gods to other men, but he is GOD to them. He lends them his name, and this is their authority for acting as judges, but they must take care that they do not misuse the power entrusted to them, for the Judge of judges is in session among them . . . There must be some government among men, and as angels are not sent to dispense it, God

---

11 Psalm 82 Bible Commentary. (n.d.). Retrieved December 03, 2017, from https://www.christianity.com/bible/commentary.php?com=wes&b=19&c=82

allows men to rule over men."[12]

However, there are a number of pointers which suggest a different interpretation—that God, in the setting of a "divine" council, is condemning angelic beings for their poor superintendence over the nations of the earth.

As evidence for this latter view, the word translated "gods" in the ESV is the Hebrew elohim, which is used in scripture to describe divine beings—both of the one true God (Genesis 1:1) and of generic divinities such as angels (Psalm 8:5) and pagan deities (Judges 11:24). It is rarely used of humans (Exodus 4:16, 7:1), though when it is context tends to suggest a metaphorical sense (for instance, the one true God made Moses to be God to Pharaoh because He spoke on behalf of God). In addition, there are various passages in the Old Testament where angels are referred to as "sons of God" (as in verse 6), such as Job 1:6, Job 38:7, Genesis 6:2, and Deuteronomy 32:8. This word usage suggests that divine and not human beings are likely in view.

"The real problem with the human view, though," according to Heiser, "is that it cannot be reconciled with other references in the Hebrew Old Testament that refer to a divine council of elohim."[13]

For instance, Psalm 89:5-11 gives a similar description of a scene wherein a congregation of holy ones are gathered about God. Heiser notes that in this passage, "God's divine council is an assembly in the heavens, not on earth"[14] on the basis of parallelistic language such as, "let the heavens praise your wonders, O Lord, your faithfulness in the assembly of the holy ones" (Psalm 89:5, ESV). This psalmist, in parallel fashion to Psalm 82, likewise informs us that none can compare to the Lord; that He has the power to crush the gods of the nations because

---

12 Psalm 82 by C. H. Spurgeon. (n.d.). Retrieved December 03, 2017, from https://www.blueletterbible.org/Comm/spurgeon_charles/tod/ps82.cfm
13 Michael S. Heiser, The Unseen Realm: Recovering the Supernatural Worldview of the Bible, Lexham Press, 2015, Kindle edition.
14 ibid.

both heaven and earth are His to take. Outside of these Psalms, similar scenes of divine beings presenting themselves to God or as part of a heavenly council are described in the first few chapters of Job and in 1 Kings 22:19-23.

This passage, therefore, seems to provide us with an important piece of background information for the next passages we'll examine in Daniel's book: the angels which God has placed over the nations are corrupt and God will one day displace them and reclaim the nations for Himself.

Daniel

The picture painted for us by scripture so far is of many nations with fallen angelic forces over them. This picture is likewise presented in the tenth chapter of the book of Daniel, written when the Persian empire had power over much of the world, including Judah. In this chapter, we learn that an angelic messenger came to Daniel in answer to a prayer that Daniel had made 3 weeks before. The angel also makes an interesting admission about his tardiness—God had heard the prayer immediately and sent the angel in response. What held him back?:

> "The prince of the kingdom of Persia withstood me twenty-one days, but Michael, one of the chief princes, came to help me, for I was left there with the kings of Persia . . ." (Daniel 10:13, ESV)

On the basis that the same Hebrew word for "prince" in prince of Persia (sar in Hebrew, archon in Greek) is also applied to Michael the archangel in this verse, and since this prince is fighting two angels, it seems safe to conclude that the prince is not an earthly power, but an angelic one (though one in opposition to God).[15] Just a few verses later, the curtain is pulled back even

---

15 William Shea argues that the use of the plural form of king at the end of this verse is meant to refer to the co-regency of Cambyses and Cyrus ("Wrestling with the Prince of Persia: A Study on Daniel 10," read at

CODY COOK

farther as we are given a glimpse of the spiritual machinations
behind the scenes of shifting hegemonic fortunes:
"now I will return to fight against the prince of Persia; and
when I go out, behold, the prince of Greece will come"
(Dan. 10:20 ESV).

It was indeed as this angel said, for the Greek empire emerged
to displace the Persian one. It seems then that all of this was
arranged by spiritual powers in opposition to God's kingdom. The
apparent clarity of this chapter's discussion of the demonic
operations underneath political and military movements led
biblical scholar Walter Wink to conclude that Daniel 10 provided
the most "notable development" in the Old Testament of "the idea
that God had appointed an angel or god over each of the pagan
nations." [16]

Unger argues that the conflict between Daniel's angel and the
angelic princes of Persia and Greece, which he views through the
lens of Ephesians 6:10-12, points to a larger conflict in which
"spirits [operate] in the realm of the governments of the satanic
world system through the human agencies of kings, princes, and
other government officials. Those demonic powers energizing and
directing their human agents are called 'the rulers of the darkness
of this world' . . . designating the character of the satanic world
system in relation to its government."[17]

This idea is not restricted only to contemporary exegetes. In his

https://digitalcommons.andrews.edu/cgi/viewcontent.cgi?article=1619&co
ntext=auss), and therefore no angelic powers behind Persia and Greece are
in view,. However, the angelic interpretation seems to make more sense in
the immediate cotext as well as in the context of the Jewish perspective on
angelic powers over nations. That being said, it also isn't implausible that
the "kings" of Persia are human kings and that Daniel has simply
connected the earthly and spiritual powers together due to the permeability
of earthly and spiritual power structures.
16 Walter Wink, Naming the Powers: The Language of Power in the New
Testament, Fortress Press, 1984, Kindle edition.
17 Merrill F. Unger, Unger's Commentary on the Old Testament Volume II:
Isaiah-Malachi, 1981, The Moody Bible Institute of Chicago, p. 1674.

commentary on Daniel, the fifth century bishop Theodoret of Cyr, linking this passage with Deuteronomy 32:8-9, understood that the prince of Persia was "the one entrusted to rule over the very king of the Persians." In *On First Principles*, Origen concludes from this section that "there are rulers over individual nations . . . who, as is clearly shown by the sense of the passage itself, are not humans but powers." The notion that this passage is grounded in the teaching of Deuteronomy 32:8-9 was affirmed by other major early church writers, including Pseudo-Dionysius and Jerome, the latter of which reasoned, "this was the angel to whose charge Persia was committed, in accordance with what we read in Deuteronomy."[18]

This notion of so-called "patron angels" in Daniel 10 gives us greater insights into other passages in the book. For instance, Daniel 2 describes a dream of Babylon's king and its interpretation by the prophet Daniel. The king saw an enormous statue separated into various parts, each made of lower quality material than the next. Its feet, made of iron and clay, were struck by a stone which was cut without hands and the statue was destroyed. This statue, Daniel explained, was a series of empires. In the days of the fourth and last kingdom, that of Rome, the God of heaven would establish a kingdom which would never be destroyed but would put an end to all earthly empires.

Daniel saw a vision paralleling this dream some years later, though he saw these kingdoms for what they truly are—great and destructive beasts which would be destroyed by the divine Son of Man when God gave dominion of the earth to the Son of Man and to His saints (Daniel 7).

A moment should be spent noting how this passage in Daniel 7 was translated into Greek versions (here we focus on the Septuagint [aka LXX], though other manuscript traditions such as

---

18 All citations from this paragraph are from Ancient Christian Commentary on Scripture: Old Testament XIII: Ezekiel, Daniel, Stevenson and Glerup ed., 2008, Intervarsity Press, Downer's Grove, p. 276-278.

Theodotion likewise make our point) which the apostles were familiar with and cited often. When the horn (or king) which emerged from the fourth beast is judged, his authority (*exousia*) is taken from him. Instead, authority (*exousia*) and rule (*arche*) is given to the people of the saints of the Most High, whose kingdom is an everlasting kingdom—and all authorities shall serve and obey Him.[19] These Greek terms are significant due to how they will be used in the New Testament literature, so they are worth noting.

When chapters 2 and 7 are taken with the data from chapter 10 which suggest "patron angels" over the nations, Daniel may be understood as speaking of two heads when it comes to corrupt earthly powers—one spiritual and the other properly earthly. And if God will judge the earthly kingdoms and their heads, he will likewise judge their heavenly powers, as Isaiah also tells us.

Isaiah

Isaiah likely gives us yet more glimpses into the demonic grounding of political power. For instance, Isaiah 24:21 speaks of God's coming judgment in a parallel fashion, relating the heavenly powers to the earthly ones:

> "On that day the LORD will punish the host of heaven, in heaven, and the kings of the earth, on the earth" (Isaiah 24:21 ESV).[20]

---

19 Ronn A. Johnson, in his 2004 dissertation The Old Testament Background for Paul's Use of "Principalities and Powers," notes that the word for authorities in the last instance is *exousia* in the LXX and *arche* in Theodotion (p. 131-132). He understands this term as used in this passage to be applied to spiritual authorities, not earthly ones. In other words, Daniel presents a future where the authority to rule will be given to the saints, which, by implication, means it is taken away from the divine council described in Psalm 82, therefore restoring God's image as authority to reign over the earth in man. As Paul asks in 1 Corinthians 6:3, "do you not know that we will judge angels?"

20 See Psalm 148:2, Joshua 5:14, Daniel 8:11, Luke 2:6, Ephesians 6:12 for identification with the angels as the "host." See also Isaiah 34:1-4.

21

In addition, it provides us with something rare in the Old Testament—a discussion of Satan. Not coincidentally, he is paralleled with a corrupt earthly ruler.

In Isaiah 14, the king of Babylon is described as an oppressor, an insolent ruler who struck the peoples in wrath with unrelenting persecution. And yet God will break the scepter of power and the grave will be stirred up to meet him. Suddenly, the language shifts and this king is described using language more fit for a rebellious angel. He is described as a shining star, one who seeks to ascend above the stars of God and make himself like the Most High, sitting in a high throne on the mount of assembly. As Heiser notes:

> "Isaiah 14 reads like an attempted coup in the divine council. [This figure] wanted his seat in the divine assembly on the divine mountain to be above all others. He wanted to be 'like the Most High' (elyon). But there can be only one of those."[21]

Though limited human vision sees such a figure as unstoppable, the divinely guided Isaiah makes this prediction of how the king will be seen by onlookers:

> "Those who see you will stare at you and ponder over you: 'Is this the man who made the earth tremble, who shook kingdoms?'" (Isa. 14:16 ESV).

Ezekiel

A strikingly similar discussion appears in Ezekiel 28. The king of Tyre is likewise described as suffering from delusions of divine grandeur. Though he pictures himself as sitting on the throne of a

---

21 Michael S. Heiser, The Unseen Realm: Recovering the Supernatural Worldview of the Bible, Lexham Press, 2015, Kindle edition. Heiser is here building upon Semitic background information that the divine mountain is the setting in Ugaritic mythology for its divine council.

god (verse 2) he is a man and will die as one:
> "Because you think you are wise, as wise as a god, I am going to bring foreigners against you, the most ruthless of nations; they will draw their swords against your beauty and wisdom and pierce your shining splendor" (Ezekiel 28:6-7, NIV)

Ezekiel is told to raise a lamentation over this king, comparing him explicitly to another figure. This figure was in Eden, the garden of God. He was an anointed guardian cherub on the holy mountain of God[22:]
> "You were in Eden, the garden of God; every precious stone adorned you . . . You were anointed as a guardian cherub, for so I ordained you. You were on the holy mount of God . . .Through your widespread trade you were filled with violence, and you sinned. So I drove you in disgrace from the mount of God, and I expelled you, guardian cherub, from among the fiery stones" (Ezekiel 28:13-16).

As a result of his unrighteousness and violence,[23] God declared that He would cast him from the mountain as a profane thing and burn him to ashes with an all-consuming fire.[24]

Though the Old Testament is otherwise sparse in its references to Satan, it is worth noting these passages in Isaiah and Ezekiel since they associate him with political power and provide useful

---

22 Note the scene being set is consistent with the setting of the divine council. Heiser's section on this passage in The Unseen Realm is worth reading for his treatment of critical scholarship which denies a reference to Satan in this passage, opting instead for an identification with Adam.
23 Recall Jesus' words in John 8:44.
24 The language here is in the past tense, perhaps suggesting an action not yet completed at the time of the writing but as good as done. Though less clear, Ezekiel 31 may provide a similar reference to Satan in comparison to Assyria by way of analogy to a great tree who was the envy of all the trees in Eden. This great tree along with its comrades will die like military men (verse 16-17). A possible connection to the fallen members of the divine council, Satan at their head, could be implied here. Note parallel language in Psalm 82.

23

connective tissue between the serpent story in Genesis chapter 3 and the New Testament.

Also relevant, though a controversial identification among some scholars (including Heiser), is the reference to the adversary (translation of the Hebrew "ha satan") in Job, a figure which accuses men before God and who describes himself as "roaming through the earth" and "walking around on it," (Job 1:7) language which Merrill argues suggests "claiming dominion over the territory being traversed."[25]

Conclusion

The Old Testament provides us with some key pieces of information which we should keep in mind as we move forward in this study. The most salient points are:

1. Though God is always sovereign ultimately, He gave up the nations of the earth into the hands of angelic beings which were corrupted.

2. Satan is presented as the prototypical rebellious angel and usurper who takes from mankind his birthright to rule over the earth. He is often compared with despots and associated with political power.

3. God points forward to a day when the kingdoms of the earth will be crushed by the kingdom of God. This kingdom would be inaugurated by the divine Son of Man and shared with his holy ones, thus bringing God's intention for man to rule over creation full circle. Until then, the kingdoms of men are guided by unseen forces which are not hospitable to humanity's best interests.

These emphases are not dropped in the intervening years between the Testaments but continue to be developed in the

---

25 Merrill F. Unger, Biblical Demonology, Kregel, 1994, Kindle edition.

Jewish imagination, as we shall now see.

FIGHT THE POWERS

2

Between the Testaments

Although intertestamental Jewish literature (the religious works written between the Old and New Testaments) is not considered scripture by Jews and most Christians, the notion of the permeability between divine powers and human nations is developed between the Old Testament and New Testament eras and affected the way that the New Testament writers understood and wrote about this theme. Therefore it will be helpful to briefly survey some of the relevant writings. Though there are various ideas in this literature which could have relevance to the topic now under examination, this chapter will focus exclusively on how the idea of "patron angels" of the nations is expressed and developed.

A significant theme in the intertestamental development of patron angels is that the angelic figures behind the nations took a keen interest in persecuting God's special people. In light of the experiences of the Jewish people during this time period—in particular their subjugation and humiliation under the Seleucid empire—it is not difficult to imagine why. In some writings, it is suggested that God allowed the persecution of the Jews to happen in order to punish them, but that in any case the demons had overstepped their bounds and would be condemned for it (see Isaiah 47:5-15 and Jeremiah 25:12 for how a similar narrative had earlier been proposed for Babylon's treatment of Judah).

This idea is possibly represented in 1 Enoch 89 (ca. 163-142 BC) where seventy shepherds (perhaps of the seventy nations in Genesis 10?) are charged with killing more of the sheep delivered up to them than God allowed, with the result that they were thrown into a flaming abyss.[26] The Hebrew Testament of Naphtali (medieval in date though Russell notes an argument from M. de Jonge that it may go back to an older text) likewise confirms the use of this number to point to angelic superintendence over the nations:

> "the Lord came down from his highest heavens, and brought down with him seventy ministering angels, Michael at their head. He commanded them to teach the seventy families which sprang from the loins of Noah seventy languages . . . But the holy language, the Hebrew language, remained only in the house of Shem and Eber." [27]

The book of Jubilees (ca. 160-150 BC) also speaks of angelic figures placed over the nations—though not Israel—with the additional detail that it is their job to misdirect them from knowing God:

> "There are many nations and many peoples, and all are

---

26 Though of unclear significance for our thesis, it is of interest that the shepherds and their sheep are described as blind in 1 Enoch 88 while the name of Sammael—identified as Satan who is over wicked angels and powers in the 1st-3rd century AD Martyrdom of Isaiah —means "the blind God."

27 D. S. Russell, The Method and Message of Jewish Apocalyptic, The Westminster Press, 1964, p. 248. See also the medieval Palestinian Targum of Genesis 11:7: "And the Lord said to the seventy angels which stand before Him, Come, we will descend and will there commingle their language, that a man shall not understand the speech of his neighbour. And the Word of the Lord was revealed against the city, and with Him seventy angels, having reference to seventy nations, each having its own language, and thence the writing of its own hand." Finally, 3 Enoch (pre to early medieval) speaks of 72 (following the LXX—see also the variations between 70 and 72 in manuscripts of Luke 10) angelic princes of kingdoms corresponding to the 72 tongues of the world (17:8) and correlates the Prince of Rome with the fallen angel Sammael and the Prince of Persia with Dubbiel (26:13).

His, and over all hath He placed spirits in authority to lead
them astray from Him. But over Israel He did not appoint
any angel or spirit, for He alone is their ruler, and He will
preserve them and require them at the hand of His angels
and His spirits, and at the hand of all His powers in order
that He may preserve them and bless them, and that they
may be His and He may be theirs from henceforth for
ever."[28]

Likewise Sirach (ca. 200-175 BC) contends that, "for in the
division of the nations of the whole earth, he appointed a ruler for
every nation, but Israel is the Lord's own portion" (Sirach 17:17,
NRSV). Though not all manuscripts include the clause before "he
appointed," the passage seems to suggest angelic rulers and not
human ones regardless. After all, Israel had human kings. If the
clause is included, then the case is even stronger that Sirach has
patron angels in mind since it seems to suggest that these rulers
were appointed at Babel.

Finally, the Qumran community likewise reflected on the
conjunction of demonic and human power, as Clinton Arnold
discussed in his *Powers of Darkness: Principalities & Powers in
Paul's Letters*:

> "The community published a document, now known as the
> War Scroll (1QM), which describes an impending battle
> between the 'children of light' and the 'children of
> darkness.' On one level 'the sons of darkness' are defined
> as the Romans (Kittim), but on another spiritual level they
> are identified with Satan and the evil angelic forces of his
> kingdom (1QM 13.4-5). When the battle occurs, it would
> be decided by the direct intervention of God, who would
> raise his hand 'in an everlasting blow against Satan and all
> the hosts of his kingdom' (1 QM 18.1). The scroll sees the
> battle taking place on two dimensions, with men fighting
> men and angels fighting angels."[29]

---

28 Cited from http://www.pseudepigrapha.com/jubilees/15.htm
29 Clinton E. Arnold, Powers of Darkness, IVP Academic, 2009, Kindle

Though Qumran was only one expression of Judaism, the underlying ideas expressed here are consistent with Old Testament teaching and intertestamental writings (as we have seen) and help to form the matrix in which the New Testament develops its own theology of political power (as we are about to see).

In summation, the intertestamental Jewish literature supports our essential readings of Genesis 10-11, Deuteronomy 32, and Daniel 10, though each writer added his own distinct interpretations.

Now we can turn to the New Testament to see how the apostles approached these concepts and built a new theology of demonic-political power in the light of Christ and His coming.

edition.

3

The New Testament

The New Testament picks up on the conjunction of earthly and spiritual powers as presented in the Old Testament and intertestamental material and gives this idea new definition in light of the coming of Christ and His victory over the powers through the cross.

The Gospels

To begin with, the Gospels confirm the notion of demonic power over the nations in the strongest possible terms. In Luke 4:5-7, Satan himself claims to have been given authority over kingdoms:

"And the devil took him up and showed him all the kingdoms of the world in a moment of time, and said to him, 'To you I will give all this authority and their glory, for it has been delivered to me, and I give it to whom I will. If you, then, will worship me, it will all be yours.'" (Luke 4:5-7, ESV).

This is stated to Jesus in His wilderness temptation and the savior does not dispute the assertion. Indeed, he explicitly affirms it in John 12:31, 14:30, and 16:11 where He calls Satan "the ruler of this world." That is not to say that Jesus saw Satan as an all-sovereign. Jesus understood that His coming heralded a new age and that even Satan and his angels would be judged as a result of it (see Mark 1:15, Luke 11:20, Matthew 25:41, and John 12:31).

What does become clear, however, is that Jesus sees the kingdom of God as so different from the kingdoms of men that being a part of it requires a complete re-orientation of kingdom methods and behaviors. When Pilate asks Jesus about His kingship, Jesus responds by saying:

> "My kingdom is not of this world. If my kingdom were of this world, my servants would have been fighting, that I might not be delivered over to the Jews. But [now] my kingdom is not from the world" (John 18:36, ESV).

Earthly kingdoms use force—they are inherently violent. They back up their demands with the threat of imprisonment, seizure of property, and even death. Jesus claims that the kingdom of God is not like that and that those who are part of it do not use the violent tools of the state. With the use of the Greek word "nun" (now), there is a suggestion that this kingdom would one day conquer the world, but that at the time He was speaking to Pilate it had not.

When, though, would it establish itself as an earthly kingdom? It seems that there are two possible answers:
1. Some time between Jesus' resurrection and His second coming through the will of men taking control of nations.
2. At His second coming.

The former possibility is problematic at best. To begin with, the Kingdom of God is singular. It will not do to speak of Christian nations, because Jesus is speaking of the one Christian nation that will some day reclaim creation completely. Christians in America, for example, cannot create a Christian nation which borders reach only from California to New York—the only true Christian nation, the kingdom of God, will be worldwide.

In addition, the idea of a kingdom of God being established through normal political means is utterly foreign to the New Testament, which assumes a church disconnected from state power (more on that later). This means that if there is to be a kingdom of God established upon the earth, it must be established by Christ Himself.

Finally, Luke chapter 10 hints at the spiritual and not political nature of the church's present conquest of the world. Jesus sends out His disciples to declare the gospel message to various towns. How many does he send? Seventy-two, of course. The same number for the nations in the Greek version of Genesis chapter 10. Careful readers might object that this number was actually 70 in the Hebrew text, and they'd be right. Copyists of Luke's Gospel noticed this as well. That's why some manuscripts of this Gospel read 70 instead. The suggestion seems to be that God had begun to reclaim the nations by the spread of the gospel message apart from physical force.

And what did Jesus see as the significance of His sending out the disciples to declare the good news? It was "the kingdom of God coming near to [them]" (verse 9) and "Satan falling like lightning from heaven" (verse 18). When the gospel goes out to the nations, it is the very kingdom of God breaking into demonic territory and the defeat of Satan.

It should be no surprise then that in Mark 13:25-26, Jesus identifies Himself with the Son of Man coming on the clouds to judge the nations in Daniel chapter 7 and connects it with the stars/powers of heaven (terms applied to angelic beings throughout scripture—see for example Job 38:6, Ephesians 1:21) falling:

> "the stars will be falling from heaven, and the powers in the heavens will be shaken. And then they will see the Son of Man coming in clouds with great power and glory" (ESV).

In summation, Christ's coming points to the beginning of God's reclaiming of the world from the demonic powers. But how?

FIGHT THE POWERS

Acts

In Acts chapter 2 we see the reality that Christ has subverted the powers expressed more subtly, though it is still quite present. The chapter begins on the first Pentecost (the Jewish festival of Harvest or Shavu'ot) after Christ's resurrection and ascension. Jesus' disciples are assembled together in one place when:

"suddenly there came from heaven a sound like a mighty rushing wind, and it filled the entire house where they were sitting. And divided tongues as of fire appeared to them and rested on each one of them. And they were all filled with the Holy Spirit and began to speak in other tongues as the Spirit gave them utterance" (Acts 2:2-4, ESV).

Though it may not be apparent at first blush, this event points back to the confusion of languages at Babel. Even on a surface reading, one can see that they are parallel, though opposite, events. At Babel, humans are cursed by a confusion of languages which divides them into various nations, each governed by an angelic power. At Pentecost, and then throughout the book of Acts, humans are blessed by being given the ability to cross language barriers to create one new "nation" in Christ which belongs to Him alone.

But beneath the surface there appear to be additional clues in the Greek to connect these two events, as Heiser argues:

"There are two key terms in the passage that connect it back to Babel in an unmistakable way. The flaming tongues are described as 'divided' (Greek: diamerizo), and the crowd, composed of Jews from all the nations, is said to have been 'confused' (Greek: suncheo). The second term, suncheo (v. 6), is the same word used in the Septuagint version of the Babel story in Genesis 11:7: 'Come, let us go down and confuse [Septuagint: suncheo] their language there.' The multiplicity of nations represented at Pentecost is another link to Babel. Each nation had a national language. More importantly, all

34

those nations referred to in Acts 2:9–11 had been disinherited by Yahweh when they were divided."[30]

Heiser highlights that the word "divided" (diamerizo) also shows up in Deuteronomy 32's presentation of Babel—"When the Most High divided [diamerizo] the nations, when he scattered humankind, he fixed the boundaries of the nations." In sum, Pentecost mirrors Babel's events (and even its vocabulary!) to communicate its reversal. What are the effects of this reversal? According to Heiser:

"As Jews gathered in Jerusalem for the celebration heard and embraced the news of Jesus and his resurrection, Jews who embraced Jesus as messiah would carry that message back to their home countries—the nations. Babel's disinheritance was going to be rectified by the message of Jesus, the second Yahweh incarnate, and his Spirit. The nations would again be his."[31]

Heiser makes another important connection between Acts 2 and the Genesis passage about Babel—their correspondence when they list the known nations of the world:

"The key idea to grasp is that the 'Table of Nations' in Genesis represents the known world at the time it was written . . . [It] lists known nations east to west, from eastern Mesopotamia to Tarshish (Gen 10: 4), the most remote western point. What lay beyond Tarshish, through what we now call the Straits of Gibraltar, was a complete mystery to the biblical writers. The list of nations in Acts 2 is not merely a rehashing of all the names in Genesis 10. Many names are different. A few observations about the list, however, reveal that it nevertheless correlates with the Table of Nations..."[32]

---

30 Michael S. Heiser, The Unseen Realm: Recovering the Supernatural Worldview of the Bible, Lexham Press, 2015, Kindle edition.
31 ibid.
32 ibid.

There is a significant exception to this correspondence, however: Tarshish, the westernmost point in Genesis 10, is missing. This explains a mystery in Paul's letter to the Romans (see Romans 15:23-28)—why he's so interested in preaching the gospel in Spain:

> "In Paul's day, Spain was where Tarshish was. Tarshish was a Phoenician colony in what was later Spain. The point is profound: Paul was convinced that his life's mission as apostle to the Gentiles—the disinherited nations—would only be finished when he got to Spain. As incredible as it sounds, Paul was conscious that his mission for Jesus actually involved spreading the gospel to the westernmost part of the known world—Tarshish—so that the disinheritance at Babel would be reversed."

In sum, the events at Pentecost signaled that God had begun to reclaim the nations disinherited at Babel by means of the initiation of a new kingdom which would conquer the world first through evangelism and finally through the return of Christ to reclaim the world.

This is why in his Pentecost sermon Peter connects Psalm 110 with the rule of Christ, arguing on the basis of it that "God has made this Jesus, whom you crucified, both Lord and Messiah" (Acts 2:36, NIV). The Psalm he is quoting speaks of the future rule of Messiah over the whole world:

> *The Lord says to my Lord:*
> *'Sit at my right hand,*
> *until I make your enemies your footstool.'*

> *The Lord sends forth from Zion your mighty scepter.*
> *Rule in the midst of your enemies! . . .*

> *The Lord is at your right hand;*
> *he will shatter kings on the day of his wrath.*
> *He will execute judgment among the nations,*
> *filling them with corpses;*
> *he will shatter chiefs over the wide earth.*

-Psalm 110:1-6, ESV

In Pentecost, therefore, we have two concepts relevant to our present study:

1. The reversal of Babel through the union of various peoples and tongues into one new humanity headed up by Christ, with the result that both demonic and earthly powers have been in some sense defeated by Christ ahead of their final judgment. Those who are God's are no longer under the authority of demons.

2. The coming physical reign of Christ on earth and the judgment of both nations and (by extension—see Psalm 82 and Isaiah 24:21) the angels in rebellion which are over them.

Later, as the apostles become convicted that the gospel message has broken down boundaries between Jew and gentile, we see Paul calling gentiles to become part of God's kingdom, thus delivering them from the relative ignorance of God which the demons over their nations kept them in. In his speech to the Athenians on Mars Hill, Paul gives a nod to the events of Babel (and perhaps also implicitly to the famous Deuteronomy 32 passage which the Jews of Paul's time saw it through) when He says that God made one humanity which was then divided into distinct nations. Though these nations did not have the direct knowledge of God afforded to Israel, they nevertheless had a sense of the divine Being whom they could strive to know more deeply:

"And he made from one man every nation of mankind to live on all the face of the earth, having determined allotted periods and the boundaries of their dwelling place, that they should seek God, and perhaps feel their way toward him and find him. Yet he is actually not far from each one of us, for 'In him we live and move and have our being'; as even some of your own poets have said, 'For we are indeed his offspring'" (Acts 17:26-29, ESV).

FIGHT THE POWERS

Because their knowledge was limited, the gentiles often failed spectacularly to understand God; but in his epistle to the Ephesians, Paul writes of the mystery finally revealed in his time, that "the Gentiles are fellow heirs, members of the same body, and partakers of the promise in Christ Jesus through the gospel" (Ephesians 3:6, ESV).

That gentiles are now united to Jews through Christ means that they were once, "alienated from the commonwealth of Israel and strangers to the covenants of promise, having no hope and without God in the world" (Ephesians 2:12). Why were they strangers to the covenants of promise? Because, "when the Most High gave to the nations their inheritance, [he] divided mankind . . . according to the number of the sons of God [but made Israel] his allotted heritage" (Deuteronomy 32:8, ESV).

This division began to be undone when God "raised [Jesus] from the dead and seated him at his right hand in the heavenly places, far above all rule [*arche*] and authority [*exousia*] and power [*dunamis*] and dominion [*kuristes*], and above every name that is named, not only in this age but also in the one to come" (Ephesians 1:20-21, ESV).

To better understand how Paul understood these rulers (*arche*) and authorities (*exousia*), we'll need to turn to a more in-depth study of his letters.

Paul's Epistles

One important component in Paul's understanding of the powers is his use of the terms, often used together, rulers (*arche*) and authorities (*exousia*). These two words bear the general meaning of rulers over geographical regions and can refer to either earthly powers or spiritual forces.

Passages where earthly powers are clearly described include Luke 12:11 where Jesus foretells that His disciples will be

38

brought before *arche* and *exousia* and Titus 3:1 where Paul encourages Christians to be subject to *arche* and *exousia*.

On the other hand, Ephesians 3:10 refers explicitly to spiritual forces when it speaks of the gospel message being made known to *arche* and *exousia* in the heavenly places. Likewise, Romans 8:38 seems clearly to use *arche* (without *exousia*) to refer to angelic powers.

However, most of the other New Testament uses of these terms fall into something of a gray area. Will Christ abolish all *arche* and *exousia* in heaven or on earth at the end of the age (1 Corinthians 15:24)? Is He now seated "in the heavenly places above all *arche* and *exousia*" in heaven or on earth (Ephesians 1:21)? Is Christ the head and creator of all *arche* and *exousia* in heaven or on the earth (Colossians 1:16, 2:10)? Indeed, did Christ's crucifixion disarm the earthly or angelic *arche* and *exousia* (Colossians 2:15)?[33]

When it comes to Paul's use of these two words in conjunction, Ronn A. Johnson builds a multi-faceted argument that we should understand them in light of their use in Daniel 7. Firstly, Daniel 7:27 is the only verse in the Greek Septuagint (also known as the LXX) where *arche* and *exousia* occur together. Secondly, Paul's

---

33 This last reference may be focusing primarily on spiritual forces since it follows Paul's exhortation to not follow after vain philosophy and the "stoicheia" (sometimes translated "elements") of the world (v. 8). Paul uses the same word in Galatians 4:3-9 and connects it with false gods. Arnold argues that:
"The interpretation of stoicheia as personal spiritual entities is the most compelling view. Consequently this interpretation has commanded the consent of the majority of commentators in the history of the interpretation of the passages. This view is based partly on the widespread usage of stoicheia for astral spirits in the second and third centuries A.D. (and probably before). The word was used, for instance, in the Greek magical papyri in connection with the Zodiac: 'I conjure you by the 12 stoicheia of heaven and the 24 stoicheia of the world in order that you would lead me to Heracles'" (Clinton E. Arnold, Powers of Darkness, IVP Academic, 2009, Kindle edition).

39

view of Christ's death as triumphing over the powers and principalities has parallels to Daniel's view of the coming of the Son of Man to judge the powers. Thirdly, the plural form "*exousian*" is only used in Daniel 3:2 and and 7:27 in the LXX and both to refer to evil rulers whose power is stripped from them, just as in 1 Corinthians 15:24-28[34]:

> "Then comes the end, when he delivers the kingdom to God the Father after destroying every rule and every authority [*archen*] and power [*exousian*]. For he must reign until he has put all his enemies under his feet . . . When all things are subjected to him, then the Son himself will also be subjected to him who put all things in subjection under him, that God may be all in all" (ESV).

If Johnson is correct about Paul being influenced here by Daniel, then there is a clear connection between God overthrowing human kingdoms in Daniel and Christ dethroning the powers in Paul. It is also worth highlighting that in both Daniel and Paul the victory is one wrought by God and not by weapons of human warfare.[35]

Indeed, Ephesians 6:12 provides us with a helpful paradigm for understanding how we should approach the spiritual powers which operate behind the flesh and blood powers which we may be tempted to focus our attacks upon. It reminds us that our fight is not really against physical powers—even if physical powers are directly oppressing us—but the spiritual powers which operate

---

34 Ronn A. Johnson, The Old Testament Background for Paul's Use of "Principalities and Powers": A Dissertation Presented to The Faculty of the Department of Bible Exposition Dallas Theological Seminary In Partial Fulfillment of the Requirements for the Degree Doctor of Philosophy, May 2004. p. 198.

35 This point brings to one's mind Psalm 33. Verse 12—"blessed is the nation who God is the LORD; and the people whom he hath chosen for his own inheritance"—is often misapplied to the United States by American evangelicals, but it precedes a more striking passage: "the king is not saved by his great army; a warrior is not delivered by his great strength. The war horse is a false hope for salvation, and by its great might it cannot rescue" (v. 16-17, ESV).

behind the scenes:
"We do not wrestle against flesh and blood, but against the rulers [*arche*], against the authorities [*exousia*], against the cosmic powers over this present darkness, against the spiritual forces of evil in the heavenly places" (Ephesians 6:12 ESV).[36]

This verse in Ephesians suggests an implicit connection between angelic and earthly authorities, and it is this connection which might account for Paul's ambiguity in other places. Note for instance in 1 Corinthians 2:6-8 the phrase "rulers of this age" (*archonton tou aionos toutou*):
"Yet among the mature we do impart wisdom, although it is not a wisdom of this age or of the rulers of this age, who are doomed to pass away. But we impart a secret and hidden wisdom of God, which God decreed before the ages for our glory. None of the rulers of this age understood this, for if they had, they would not have crucified the Lord of glory" (ESV).

Did Paul have in mind fallen angels who sought to crucify Christ not knowing that they were sealing their own fate? Or might it be that he was condemning human rulers for their immorally-motivated ignorance in murdering God Himself? Compare this passage to Paul's words in Acts 13:27, which indict

---

36 With this in mind, we can understand Paul's advice to put down sword and gun to take up weapons of a different nature:
"For though we walk in the flesh, we are not waging war according to the flesh. For the weapons of our warfare are not of the flesh but have divine power to destroy strongholds" (2 Corinthians 10:3-4, ESV).

For Paul, physical kingdoms are not our primary obstacle. As opposed to the Jewish Zealots of his era, he did not see taking up arms against Caesar as an effective way to combat the powers which hold God's people in bondage. Indeed, if you kill one Caesar another will merely rise up to take his place. But if the power behind the power could be defeated, then you've really accomplished something. As the lyrics to Sydney Carter's The George Fox Song tell us, "you can't kill the devil with a gun or a sword."

41

human rulers for their slaying of the Messiah:

> "For those who live in Jerusalem and their rulers, because they did not recognize him nor understand the utterances of the prophets, which are read every Sabbath, fulfilled them by condemning him" (ESV).

This parallel passage suggests a human culprit in 1 Corinthians, as does the verse immediately preceding 1 Corinthians 2:6-8 which speaks of "the wisdom of men," though this isn't the only word on the subject. For instance, the fourth century Pauline commentator Ambrosiaster argued that the "rulers of this age" were not the Jewish rulers—because they were subject to the Romans—and not the Romans—since "Pilate himself said that he found no fault in him."—"The rulers who crucified him were the demons. They knew that Jesus was the Messiah but not that He was the Son of God, and so it can be said that they crucified him in ignorance."[37]

Regardless of whether 1 Corinthians 2:6-8 is referring to human rulers of this age or demonic ones, we are left with the same result: Satan worked to bring about the crucifixion event which humans carried out (John 13:27, Revelation 12:4), so there is complicity shared between both human and spiritual beings in this event.

So, when can we be sure that Paul is using *arche* and *exousia* to refer to human powers and when are spiritual powers clearly in view? Sometimes context makes one or another identification obvious. However, it may not always be the case that only one referent is intended. In much of the intertestamental literature (and throughout the Old Testament but especially in Daniel chapter 10's discussion of the Prince of Persia), there is an

---

37 Ancient Christian Commentary on Scripture: New Testament VII: 1-2 Corinthians, Bray ed., 1999, Intervarsity Press, Downers Grove, p. 22. See also the early Christian writing The Ascension of Isaiah, which says of the prophecy of the virgin conceiving: "(this) hath escaped all the heavens and all the princes and all the gods of this world" (11:16, http://www.earlychristianwritings.com/text/ascension.html).

earthly/heavenly conjunction when it comes to the powers. Perhaps for Paul there is no separating the two types of powers—they are not mutually exclusive but blend together.

So, for instance, when Paul writes, "then comes the end, when [Jesus] delivers the kingdom to God the Father after destroying every rule and every authority and power. For he must reign until he has put all his enemies under his feet" (1 Corinthians 15:24-25 ESV), he could have easily had in mind both physical kingdoms and their spiritual authorities, particularly since it is true that Christ will in fact destroy both types, as is evident in the other biblical material we've surveyed.

After examining the language of *arche* and *exousia* in both Paul and in the Greek Old Testament which influenced his use of those terms, Johnson concluded that:
> "First, the powers of Paul and the powers of the Old Testament are similar in character; they are spirits which are antagonistic to the temporal causes of God and his people. Second, the two groups of powers are similar in role; both are given temporary rule of humans on earth according to the ultimate pleasure of Yahweh. Third, both groups of powers suffer the same destiny; in the end they will have their rule taken from them and they will be punished."[38]

Though some scholars have questioned that Paul ever had spiritual powers in mind when he used these terms,[39] it seems hard to avoid such a conclusion, particularly if one holds to Pauline authorship of all of the canonical books attributed to him.

---

38 Ronn A. Johnson, The Old Testament Background for Paul's Use of "Principalities and Powers": A Dissertation Presented to The Faculty of the Department of Bible Exposition Dallas Theological Seminary In Partial Fulfillment of the Requirements for the Degree Doctor of Philosophy, May 2004.

39 See for instance Carr's Angels and Principalities, which argues for human referents in every instance of these words in Paul's letters but the most unavoidable, which he simply explains away as pseudo-Pauline.

Keeping in mind the Old Testament and intertestamental Jewish understanding of the permeability of demonic and human authority which influenced Paul, along with the ambiguity of Paul's use of terms like *arche* and *exousia*, it seems reasonable to conclude that when Paul speaks of Christ undermining powers and authorities through His crucifixion and resurrection (and destroying them fully when He comes again), he generally had both types of power in mind. We can add to our list of reasons a point made in the previous section—that Paul was steeped in the apostolic understanding that God was defeating the powers by reclaiming the nations from the demons to create a new kingdom under Christ.

Paul's Epistle to the Roman Church

Because one passage in this letter (chapter 13, though it should not be read separately from what precedes it in chapter 12) is given a great deal of prominence amongst supporters of church and state unification, it seemed appropriate to treat it separately from the rest of what we read in Paul's extant writings.

The key verse which is often discussed in this passage is 13:1—"Let every person be subject to the governing authorities [*exousia*]" (ESV). Though Dibelius and Cullman suggested a double reference for *exousia* in Romans 13, Carr (in his 1981 *Angels and Principalities: The Background, Meaning, and Development of the Pauline Phrase Hai Archai Kai Hai Exousiai*) makes a persuasive case that only earthly powers, not angelic ones, were the intended referent for this word. If there is a double meaning here, Paul doesn't give us strong contextual basis for supposing so. However, that doesn't mean that there aren't other possible allusions to the notion of demonic powers in this passage.

Paul writes in chapter 13 that Christians should be subject to the state because authorities are instituted by God and carry the sword to avenge against those who do evil. Even taken at face value, this is not an endorsement for blurring the lines between church and state since the preceding verses in chapter 12 distinguish what the state does—use force against its enemies—from how Christians are expected to behave:

> "Beloved, never avenge yourselves, but leave it to the wrath of God, for it is written, 'Vengeance is mine, I will repay, says the Lord.' . . . Do not be overcome by evil, but overcome evil with good" (Rom. 12:19-21 ESV).

If the state is an "avenger" for God (13:4), the Christian is told to be the opposite—to never avenge but leave room for God's wrath, exercised either on the day of judgment or vicariously through state violence against the wicked. Instead of participating in this state violence, the Christian is called to overcome evil with good. That point should be enough to answer those who are in favor of uniting the powers of church and state, but there are secondary points which may provide additional support for our thesis.

For instance, it should be observed that Paul's statement about God's vengeance is a quotation from Deuteronomy 32:35—from the same passage which gave us the first glimpse of the angelic powers over the nations.[40] In the context of Deuteronomy 32:35,

---

40 As a reminder, this passage was well-known at Paul's time for its teaching that God had given the nations over to angelic beings while choosing Israel as His special portion. In the new covenant, it is the church which is God's special portion and its members are citizens of His kingdom. We may be encouraged by Paul to, "pray for rulers and for all who have authority so that we can have quiet and peaceful lives full of worship and respect for God" (1 Timothy 2:2, ESV), but we are not encouraged to think of ourselves as a people under the authority of two kingdoms. We are sojourners in a kingdom held by demons and should conduct ourselves as respectful guests. But we are in truth citizens and ambassadors of a different kingdom. It will not do to declare allegiance to a kingdom which is opposed to the one we are claiming to represent, particularly when the kingdom of God will smash the kingdoms of men (Daniel 7), will punish corrupted powers in the heavens as well as rulers on earth (Isaiah 24:21), and since even now Christ's cross has disarmed the powers (Col 2:15).

God is speaking about punishing the pagan nations for their wickedness and mocking their gods who could not protect them: "For they are a nation void of counsel, and there is no understanding in them . . . For their rock is not as our Rock; our enemies are by themselves . . .Vengeance is mine, and recompense, for the time when their foot shall slip; for the day of their calamity is at hand, and their doom comes swiftly" (Deuteronomy 32:28-35, ESV).

The immediate context of the verse that Paul cited speaks of God executing vengeance over disobedient and immoral pagan kingdoms, like Rome was in Paul's day—meaning that Paul was quoting a passage which seems to claim the opposite of what he was using it for. Is it possible that Paul was speaking in coded language to knowledgeable Christians who understood their Bibles even as he disguised his message from hostile earthly powers who might get their hands on this letter? Was Paul's real point that Christians are not actually subjects of the empire and that the kingdom in which they had their true citizenship would one day destroy the corrupt kingdoms of men for mishandling their sacred responsibilities? Perhaps Paul's point was that those in power *are* responsible for punishing the guilty and not the innocent, but their failure to do so meant that God would hold them accountable when He issued his final judgment against the powers.[41]

There are more clues that Paul may have been intending this section to be read on more than one level. For instance, the idea that "rulers are a not a terror to good conduct," and "do what is good, and you will receive [their] approval" (ESV) not only sounds hopelessly naive, but it also flies in the face of what Paul

---

41 Further evidence that Romans 12-13 should be read in light of Deuteronomy 32 may be found in the former re-purposing the latter's language. In the Greek Septuagint translation of Deuteronomy 32:41-42, God's hand holds fast to judgment (*krimatos*); His sword (*maxairan*) will devour the flesh of the rulers (*archonton*) of pagan enemies. But in Romans 13:2-4, those who resist pagan rulers will incur judgment (*krima*) since rulers (*archontes*) do not bear the sword (*maxairan*) in vain.

himself knew and experienced.

To begin with, Paul was a Jew in a land which had been occupied by a series of pagan oppressors. In addition, the epistle to the Romans was written in the mid-50s, meaning that Paul's experience of being unjustly beaten with rods by magistrates in Philippi (see Acts 16) and his public shaming of those same magistrates was more than five years in the past. Not only that, but prior to his conversion he had been given the authority to oppress and kill Christians, a charge which he now understood to be wicked. After his conversion, he would have understood that his sinless Lord and savior had been crucified by the very rulers whom he claimed "are not a terror to good conduct."

He was also a devout Jew who knew his Bible. He was familiar with stories of Pharaohs and Persian bureaucrats seeking to annihilate his people, of pagan kings being used by God to punish the Jewish people but who went further than God had desired, and of the angelic sons of God who had used their power to persecute the poor.

There is no doubt that Paul was aware of the fact that power is often corrupt and does not do what it is supposed to do, both because of human ambition and demonic influence. This suggests one of two possibilities, though they aren't mutually exclusive—Paul may have been expressing a best case scenario of what rulers *ought* to do, though often do not, or, as T. L. Carter suggested, he may have been writing ironically.

Carter establishes the use of irony as a writing practice in the ancient world and also gives a rationale for its use in this passage—to communicate a message to a specific audience which the authorities, if they had gotten hold of the letter, would not have perceived. The authorities would have been flattered by this rose-tinted portrait of themselves, though many in Paul's intended audience would have known that in practice, and in the passages which Paul cited as proof texts, those in power often do not behave in such a way.[42]

Carter also notes that defenders of the traditional view of this passage highlight parallels between it and the deutero-canonical book of Wisdom, which claims that dominion is given to rulers by God. But if this is the inspiration for Paul's words here, it ought to be read in its context:

> "Because authority was given you by the Lord and sovereignty by the Most High, who shall probe your works and scrutinize your counsels! Because, though you were ministers of his kingdom, you did not judge rightly, and did not keep the law, nor walk according to the will of God. Terribly and swiftly he shall come against you, because severe judgment awaits the exalted—For the lowly may be pardoned out of mercy but the mighty shall be mightily put to the test" (Wisdom 6:3-6, NABRE).

That Paul would allude to yet another writing to support a contention which it actually contradicts also suggests that Paul was writing with his tongue in his cheek.

Finally, Carter argues that Paul's injunction in Romans 12, to show love and mercy to one's enemies, is the true grounding for Paul's advice to Christians to honor the magistrate in chapter 13. Indeed, if the rulers had behaved as their enemy, what good would rebellion have done? They had no hope of destroying the empire with force, but more than that, "it would have entailed being overcome by evil, rather than overcoming evil with good."[43] If it was the duty of the magistrate to reward those who do good, and he instead punished them, he would likewise be punished by God for abusing his authority. If the Christian whom he oppressed responded with love to his oppression and threats, this could shame him into changing his behavior. If not, it would only compound the judgment against him. In any case, the responsibility of the Christian was to keep doing good regardless

---

42 T.L. Carter, The Irony of Romans 13, Novum Testamentum XLVI, 3
43 ibid

of the consequences—even if the laws of man forbade them from doing so:

> "But Peter and the apostles answered, 'We must obey God rather than men'" (Acts 5:29, ESV).

In summation, Paul could not have meant in Romans 12-13 that the magistrate always does what is good or even that he should *always* be obeyed. In point of fact, the external literature which Paul alludes to teaches that God would judge the state for mishandling its duties. In the mean time, the responsibility of Christians is to be beyond reproach, eschewing violence for love that either shames the oppressor or compounds the coming judgment against him.

The Book of Revelation

John's vision opens (in chapters 4 and 5) with a scene in heaven. Twenty-four thrones are assembled around God's throne. This is a vision of the divine council and it signals that the events which will be described in this book are connected to an unseen spiritual reality.[44]

If the John who wrote Revelation also wrote the Gospel and epistles which bear his name, then we can point to an interesting preoccupation for this author which will find its most detailed expression in the Revelation. John 12:31, 14:30, and 16:11 quote Jesus as saying that Satan is "the ruler of this world." 1 John 5:19 claims that the *whole world* lies under the power of Satan. Likewise Revelation 12:3 presents a dragon (Satan) with seven (seven signifying complete or total in biblical symbolism) heads with seven crowns (crowns meaning power, authority, or rule), suggesting that Satan has full power over the nations.[45] The bad

---

44 See for example our previous discussion of Psalm 82.
45 "For the universal empire of the beast, cf. Mark 4:6 where Satan offers to Christ universal domination if he worships the tempter." (J. Massyngberde Ford, The Anchor Bible: Revelation Introduction, Translation and Commentary, 1975, Doubleday & Company, Inc.)

news for him is that a woman was chosen to give birth to a Savior who would one day rule over all the nations, therefore overthrowing his power (12:5). It is no surprise then that he stood before the woman in labor, waiting to devour her child (12:4).

This description of the dragon waiting to destroy the child also points to the conjunction of earthly and demonic power, as the fourth century Donatist writer Tyconius wrote in his Commentary on the Apocalypse:

> "It was [the devil] who inflamed Herod with the fire of envy so that he would feign to adore the Christ even while seeking with all his power to kill Christ whom he knew was to be born king of the Jews."[46]

After this, there is a great war in heaven where Satan and his angels are cast out of the divine council:

> "Now war arose in heaven, Michael and his angels fighting against the dragon. And the dragon and his angels fought back, but he was defeated, and there was no longer any place for them in heaven. And the great dragon was thrown down, that ancient serpent, who is called the devil and Satan, the deceiver of the whole world—he was thrown down to the earth, and his angels were thrown down with him. And I heard a loud voice in heaven, saying, 'Now the salvation and the power [*dunamis*] and the kingdom of our God and the authority [*exousia*] of his Christ have come, for the accuser of our brothers has been thrown down, who accuses them day and night before our God. And they have conquered him by the blood of the Lamb and by the word of their testimony, for they loved not their lives even unto death'" (Revelation 12:7-11, ESV).

There has been much debate over when this war in heaven is to have taken place. Was it a primordial event before the creation of

---

46 Ancient Christian Commentary on Scripture: New Testament XII: Revelation, Weinrich ed., 2005, Intervarsity Press, Downers Grove, p. 177

Adam and Eve? Will it take place in the end times? Since in the narrative the war follows the dragon's attempt to kill the infant Jesus through Herod's machinations, and since Jesus' death and resurrection constitute a victory over Satan along with the powers and principalities which are under him, one persuasive reading is that the war and expulsion is related to Christ's victory over the powers on the cross (see John 12:31-33)—though Jesus also suggests (in Luke 10:18) that this victory may have taken place at the time of the preaching of the gospel of the kingdom.

In any case, said victory does not entail that Satan and the powers have been finally prevented from exercising dominion and influence over the nations. Revelation 12:17 tells us that after the war the dragon turned his attention toward the church, seeking to make war with it. Revelation 13:2-8 tells us how he does so: Satan still has authority over every tribe, people, language, and nation and he gives (*has given? Will give?*) this authority to a nation described as a conglomeration of the beasts in Daniel chapter 7:

> "And the beast that I saw was like a leopard; its feet were like a bear's, and its mouth was like a lion's mouth. And to it the dragon gave his power [*dunamis*] and his throne and great authority [*exousia*] . . . And they worshiped the dragon, for he had given his authority [*exousia*] to the beast, and they worshiped the beast, saying, 'Who is like the beast, and who can fight against it?' . . . Also it was allowed to make war on the saints and to conquer them. And authority [*exousia*] was given it over every tribe and people and language and nation, and all who dwell on earth will worship it, everyone whose name has not been written before the foundation of the world in the book of life of the Lamb who was slain" (ESV).[47]

This beast persecutes the people of God and seeks to create a

---

47 Compare this to our discussion of the LXX of Daniel chapter 7 where the final beast's *arche* and *exousia* is taken from him and given to the saints of the most high.

global kingdom overseen by Satan with echoes of Babel. As for its ultimate fate, we read:

> "And I saw the beast and the kings of the earth with their armies gathered to make war against him who was sitting on the horse [Jesus] and against his army. And the beast was captured [and] thrown alive into the lake of fire that burns with sulfur. And the rest were slain by the sword that came from the mouth of him who was sitting on the horse, and all the birds were gorged with their flesh" (Revelation 19:19-20, ESV).

In the narrative, Satan is then captured and bound for a thousand years, sparked by Christ's coming in judgment against the beast. There is of course an old and rather complicated debate about whether this thousand years is literal or symbolic which cannot be fully treated here. However, since it could impact the central theme of this book, it should be treated, even if briefly.

Pre-millennialists believe that Christ will return to judge the great beast and will Himself initiate a millennium of peace. This is perhaps the approach which fits most neatly with our thesis that there cannot be a true union of church and state prior to Christ's second coming, though ironically many of those who have sought to bring church and state closer together have been pre-millennialists.

Post-millennialists claim that the church will one day create a new and glorious world order, thus binding Satan, which will culminate in Christ's return. This view seems inconsistent with Christ's teaching (as well as Peter and Paul's) that the kingdom is not of this world and therefore does not use the tools and methods of worldly kingdoms. Since Christians are commanded to live out a very different kingdom mentality, the notion of a pre-advent theocratic state can never get off the ground. There is also an apparent inconsistency between the notion of a pure Christian state and human depravity, particularly in the more dominant Calvinistic forms of post-millennialism.

Amillennialists argue that the millennium is simply a way of designating the "church age" which began at Christ's ascension or perhaps at Pentecost—Satan is bound in one sense, therefore, by the spread of the gospel and the kingdom of God having broken in upon the kingdoms of men. However, Christ's millennial reign is still different in kind from the reigns of earthly kingdoms—as is evident from the plain fact that for the first three hundred years of this symbolic millennium the church had no political power whatsoever. Indeed, amillennialists do not hold, nor is it by any means evident, that the demonic realm no longer impacts the affairs of men. Peter tells us post-Pentecost that Satan goes about like a roaring lion waiting to devour his prey—namely us (1 Peter 5:8). If our enemy is now bound as a result of the kingdom of God breaking in upon the world (see Matthew 12:26-29) he must be bound only in certain respects, and perhaps even then not completely. Amillennialists have traditionally understood that Satan is bound in relation to stopping the spread of the gospel— and indeed it has spread far and wide since Jesus' ascension; but even they would not make this claim absolutely. The gospel message has not always prevailed in all places. Regions which were once predominantly Christian are now broadly secular or Muslim. Just so, it is also clear that even though Paul believed that Jesus had defeated the powers and principalities, they still remain intact until Christ's second coming (1 Corinthians 15:24).

It seems that despite our differences on the millennium, there is regardless a "now and not yet" quality to Christ's victory over the demonic.

These debates aside, Satan's fascination with political power remains unabated despite his being bound. After the millennium, the book of Revelation tells us that Satan will be released and again seek to join himself to political power, though this attempt at a coup will be short-lived:

> "Satan will be released from his prison and will come out to deceive the nations that are at the four corners of the earth, Gog and Magog, to gather them for battle; their number is like the sand of the sea. And they marched up

over the broad plain of the earth and surrounded the camp of the saints and the beloved city, but fire came down from heaven and consumed them, and the devil who had deceived them was thrown into the lake of fire and sulfur where the beast [was], and they will be tormented day and night forever and ever" (Revelation 20:7-10, ESV).

Finally, with Satan's influence removed, the nations of the earth will be under the authority of God alone. The oppression, war, and corruption of the previous age will come to an end. Our present age is so thoroughly disconnected from the one to come that John describes it in terms of starkest difference—as a new heavens and new earth:

"Then I saw a new heaven and a new earth, for the first heaven and the first earth had passed away, and the sea was no more. And I saw the holy city, new Jerusalem, coming down out of heaven from God, prepared as a bride adorned for her husband. And I heard a loud voice from the throne saying, 'Behold, the dwelling place of God is with man. He will dwell with them, and they will be his people, and God himself will be with them as their God. He will wipe away every tear from their eyes, and death shall be no more, neither shall there be mourning, nor crying, nor pain anymore, for the former things have passed away" (Revelation 21:1-4, ESV).

This will be a glorious day, indeed. But how shall we live now?

CODY COOK

FIGHT THE POWERS

PART 2

Toward a Biblical Model of Political Engagement

FIGHT THE POWERS

"But your flag decal won't get you into Heaven anymore
They're already overcrowded from your dirty little war
Now Jesus don't like killin', no matter what the reason's for
And your flag decal won't get you into Heaven anymore"
- John Prine,
"Your Flag Decal Won't Get You Into Heaven Anymore"

FIGHT THE POWERS

4

What Is the Role of Government?

The Bible in no place specifies any particular man-made political system as the one which God favors, though it is clear that He is sovereign over all kings, all governments, and all nations. Indeed, "there is no authority except from God" (Romans 13:1) and "He removes and sets up kings" (Daniel 2:21).

However, scripture does give us both the benefits and drawbacks of centralized authority. We are told in Judges 21:25 that the wickedness of Israel stemmed from their not having a monarch to organize their moral chaos. On the other hand, 1 Samuel 8:10-18 also records the warning of God that a king will confiscate the property of the people and make war using their sons as canon fodder.

In the case of Israel, monarchy was actually chosen not by God but by the people. Both God and the prophet Samuel warned Israel against this act. These data are at the very least consistent with the classical liberal viewpoint that kings emerge on the basis of the consent (even if "consent" is extorted by threats of violence) of a larger populace.

In addition, the notion of a chosen family fit to rule is somewhat undermined by scripture. For instance, though God does preserve the Davidic family in the southern kingdom of Judah in anticipation of the Davidic king Jesus, He also blesses righteous kings not of David's line in the northern kingdom of Israel even as He overthrows wicked kings and their dynasties.

The first king mentioned in the Bible is Nimrod (see Genesis chapter 10), who is described as a mighty warrior. This suggests that his throne was consolidated by force. It is stated that one of the first centers of his kingdom was in Shinar (in Genesis 10:10), where the Tower of Babel was built to consolidate human power. This attempt was thwarted by God via His sending a confusion of languages upon humanity to limit the unification of political hegemony.

Scripture therefore presents earthly authority as something of a necessary evil. It serves a divinely instituted purpose, but it comes with a great many drawbacks. The books of Kings and Chronicles are filled with stories of good kings who bless Israel and Judah as well as bad kings who oppress the people and lead them into moral depravity. God's judgment always follows.

Indeed, scripture records that God is particularly keen to judge kings and nations for their oppression of the poor and weak:
> "Hear the word of the Lord to you, king of Judah . . . : Do what is just and right. Rescue from the hand of the oppressor the one who has been robbed. Do no wrong or violence to the foreigner, the fatherless or the widow, and do not shed innocent blood in this place . . . If you do not obey these commands, declares the Lord, I swear by myself that this palace will become a ruin" (Jeremiah 22:2-5, NIV).

These guidelines, though applied here to the king of the Judahite theocracy, are also expected to be followed by pagan kings. However, it should be noted that God's expectations of secular governments differ from the expectations He had for the now defunct Israelite theocracy.

For instance, in Amos we find oracles against both Israel and her pagan neighbors. But while Israel was held accountable for not following Torah (the law of Moses), the nations were chastised for violating more basic, naturally understood directives of human decency. Gaza kidnapped people and sold them as slaves, Amon ripped open pregnant women to extend its borders, but Judah rejected the law of God and worshiped idols.[48]

So, we know what a government should not do—oppress those in need and punish the innocent. What then, ideally, *will* a government do? According to Romans 13 and 1 Peter 2:14, it will punish the evildoer while commending and rewarding those who do good. In other words, they maintain justice and social order. How precisely this is to be carried out is a matter of great disagreement among various political philosophies and parties.

Two Modern Views of Statecraft

Our modern western notions of left and right wing are typified in the late 18th century debates between the conservative Edmund Burke and the liberal Thomas Paine. Paine supported the radical revolution in France whereas Burke thought it best to make changes slowly and respect the guideposts our ancestors had planted.

Burke wrote of the danger of radical progressivism, that:
"their principles always go to the extreme . . . [they will] push for the more perfect, which cannot be attained

---

48　The Judeo-Christian tradition has always understood different ethical directives for different groups on the basis of the extent of their knowledge or calling. For instance, the Tosefta and the Talmud argued for seven laws of Noah (the Noahide laws) which gentiles are expected to abide by in contrast to the 613 that Jews are held to. Likewise Christian philosophers have argued for a "natural revelation" of God apart from scripture that pagans are condemned for disobeying. In Amos, pagan despots are not condemned for disobeying Torah or even worshiping idols, but for failing in their duties to serve justice to those at their mercy and under their authority.

63

without tearing to pieces the whole contexture of the commonwealth."[49]

Burke was undoubtedly correct when he asserted that a revolution, particularly once institutionalized, will tend toward an even greater authoritarianism than that which it replaced. Paine should have understood this all too clearly after narrowly escaping being executed while in a French jail on the charge of not being sufficiently radical.

At the same time, Paine was undoubtedly correct in his critique of Burke's unyielding traditionalism when he wrote against, "associating [precedents] with a superstitious reverence for ancient things, as monks show relics and call them holy."[50] Indeed, some precedents—such as institutionalized racism and cruelty—cry out to be broken.

Another way to understand left and right is by reflecting upon the two forces which they see in conflict. The conservative sees the political realm as a struggle between order and chaos whereas the liberal sees it as a struggle between oppressor and oppressed, particularly in the case of more radical leftists like Karl Marx.[51]

In contemporary American political debate, we could place these filters on issues such as gay marriage or police relations with minority communities. The conservative sees gay marriage through the lens of the dichotomy of a traditional order and a liberalizing chaos which threatens to rip apart the very foundation of civilized society—the family. The liberal, conversely, sees the opposing sides as a privileged class attempting to oppress an underprivileged class by hoarding rights and benefits for themselves on the basis of bigotry. On the issue of police relations with minority communities, the right sees police as the enforcers

---

49 Yuval Levin, The Great Debate: Edmund Burke, Thomas Paine, and the Birth of Right and Left, New York: Basic Books, 2014, Kindle edition.
50 Thomas Paine, The Rights of Man, Kindle edition.
51 This helpful distinction is brought out by the economist Arnold Kling in his 2017 book The Three Languages of Politics.

of moral order and those whom they use violence against as agents of chaos and crime seeking to disrupt civilized society. In contrast, the left sees these same parties as the enforcement wing of an oppressive class holding down an oppressed class of people.

That isn't to say that the lines between the dichotomies are impermeable. Black liberation theologian James Cone claimed that ethnically white people could "become black" by shedding their privilege and identifying with the oppressed (or, as Cone calls it, "joining God in the work of liberation"[52]), perhaps in a fashion akin to Christ letting go of His divine privileges to die the death of a condemned criminal on behalf of an entire race of condemned criminals. Similarly, it is not uncommon to hear conservative white Americans claim that they are not racist when they criticize other ethnic groups, but simply expect those who are different from them to behave in the same ways that they do—to "act white," as the less politically correct might phrase it.

Though the progressive dichotomy of oppressor/oppressed may resonate at points with scripture (recall that Mary's announcement of the gospel included praising God because, "He has brought down rulers from their thrones but has lifted up the humble" [Luke 1:52, NIV]), it is not ultimately adequate because it, like the conservative model, is predicated on separating society into two opposing classes of people—one of which must be reacted to with violence if justice is to be done.[53]

More than that, both models, though perhaps valid in certain circumstances, define the good on the basis of either tradition (privileging the ruling class) or progress (privileging the ruled class) instead of on the basis of universal values and the unified nature of humanity—a humanity unified both in our sin and in the solution to our sin in Christ. If our politics is focused upon siding

---

52 James Cone, A Black Theology of Liberation, New York: Orbis Books, 2010, Kindle edition.
53 Progressivism is perhaps even more open to this danger since it often bases justice on the revenge instinct and is constantly looking to overthrow some newly theorized ancient aristocracy.

with the under-privileged, it ought to be with the intention of treating them with the dignity that the privileged are treated with—not to bring the privileged down to their level with force so that we all (those of us left alive) may stand in bread lines together. The former recognizes the inherent value in all human beings made in God's image and for whom Christ died. The latter is, and historically has always been, the path to overwhelming and collective murder[54].

If both of these approaches have their problems, are Christians nevertheless obligated to choose one? In the previous century, Christian politics in America went through two major transformations. The first was from a broadly politically progressive faith to a somewhat politically detached one due to the rise of secularism as typified in the events of the Scopes monkey trial. For decades evangelicalism in particular was marked by a deep suspicion of political power. To give just one example, Merrill Unger, a once Baptist but later independent fundamentalist Bible scholar greatly respected in religiously conservative circles, wrote in his 1952 book on demonology that:

> "This world-system, nevertheless, is dominated by Satanic principles, and is beneath its deceptive veneer a seething cauldron of national and international ambitions, and commercial rivalries. Satan and his elaborately organized hierarchy of evil (Dan. 10:13; Eph. 6:12) are often the invisible agents, and the real motivating power and intelligence behind the dictators, kings, presidents, and governors, who are the visible rulers. Armed force and periodic wars, with wholesale murder and violence, are its indispensable concomitants."

Such a statement would likely be considered unpatriotic and radically anti-authoritarian in many Baptist and fundamentalist circles today.

The next transformation, from broadly politically uninvolved to

---

54 To borrow a phrase from the German filmmaker Werner Herzog.

broadly politically conservative, found its footing upon the purported right (under the banner of religious freedom) of Christian colleges like Bob Jones University to discriminate against students of color while receiving tax exemptions. The Christian Right was finally consolidated by bringing evangelicals over to the pro-life movement (a movement from which we had been conspicuously absent when the decision of Roe v Wade came down in 1973) and was further fortified over concerns related to rising secularism and popular acceptance of homosexuality.[55]

Such rapid shifts on public policy from American Christians in such a short time might suggest that scripture doesn't give us anything to stand on when it comes to how we ought to view the state and interact with it. However, there are some railings we can place around the issue of political involvement to help us to navigate this rough terrain more biblically.

---

55 Historian Randall Balmer makes this case quite strongly in his May 27, 2014 Politico article "The Real Origins of the Religious Right" (https://www.politico.com/magazine/story/2014/05/religious-right-real-origins-107133_full.html), though other accounts, such as Daniel K. Williams book *God's Own Party: The Making of the Christian Right,* gives a fuller and somewhat more nuanced treatment of the issue.

FIGHT THE POWERS

5

The Christian's Relationship

to the State

Over the centuries various models have been proposed for the proper relationship of church and state. I've consolidated most of these views under two headings—the early church/Anabaptist view and the medieval/Christendom view—so that we can assess their broad strokes in light of what we've seen so far in scripture.

Early Church/Anabaptist Model

In the early church/Anabaptist model, the two spheres of church and state cannot be joined together without one being destroyed by the other. In particular, these groups focused on the inconsistency of Christians in occupations where they would have to kill or consent to the killing of others. Though it has been popular among those holding to a Christendom view to argue that Christians in the early church who would not serve in the military refused to do so purely on the basis that it required a pagan act of worship to Caesar, the writings of the early church fathers suggest a primarily different concern—that violence is never appropriate for followers of Christ.

Justin Martyr wrote in his First Apology (ca. 150 A.D.) that Isaiah's prophecy of soldiers beating their swords into implements of agriculture and nation not lifting up sword against nation "[came] to pass" when the apostles proclaimed the gospel to every race of men with the result that "we who formerly used to murder one another . . . refrain from making war upon our enemies."[56]

Within about 30 years Irenaeus gave the same interpretation of this prophecy adding that Christians "are now unaccustomed to fighting, but when smitten, offer also the other cheek."[57]

Writing somewhere around the turn of the third century, Tertullian likewise challenged the notion that Christians could be soldiers:

> "Shall it be held lawful to make an occupation of the sword, when the Lord proclaims that he who uses the sword shall perish by the sword? And shall the son of peace take part in the battle when it does not become him even to sue at law? And shall he apply the chain, and the prison, and the torture, and the punishment, who is not the avenger even of his own wrongs? . . . And shall he keep guard before the temples which he has renounced [and] shall he diligently protect by night those whom in the day-time he has put to flight by his exorcisms, leaning and resting on the spear the while with which Christ's side was pierced? Shall he carry a flag, too, hostile to Christ?"[58]

To give only one more example out of many which are available, The Apostolic Tradition, a 3rd century church order attributed to Hippolytus, gave this guidance for Christians regarding military work:

> "A military man in authority must not execute men. If he is ordered, he must not carry it out . . . The catechumen or faithful who wants to become a soldier is to be rejected,

56 Justin Martyr, First Apology, ch. 39, accessed at
    https://en.wikisource.org/wiki/Ante-
    Nicene_Christian_Library/The_First_Apology_of_Justin_Martyr
57 Irenaeus, Against Heresies, Book IV, Chapter 34, accessed at
    http://www.newadvent.org/fathers/0103434.htm
58 Tertullian, The Chaplet, or De Corona, Kindle edition.

for he has despised God. A Christian must not become a soldier, unless he is compelled by a chief bearing the sword. He is not to burden himself with the sin of blood. But if he has shed blood, he is not to partake of the mysteries, unless he is purified by a punishment, tears, and wailing. He is not to come forward deceitfully but in the fear of God."[59]

Particularly since the state's primary tool of enforcement is violence and the threat of violence, tools which the Christian may never take up, most of the early church (virtually all of its theologians whose work is extant, though evidence of some Christians in the army exists from this period) along with the later Anabaptist tradition argued for strict separation between the two. And this was for good reason. As Douglas John Hall wrote:

"Surely Jesus as he is presented in the Synoptics and John never dreamt of anything remotely resembling the Holy Roman Empire or the United States of America as a Christian nation. I cannot even attribute such a thing to Paul, or Irenaeus, or Tertullian, or the second-century apologists . . . as for power, [the church] had none beyond its own internal persuasiveness."[60]

---

59 Apostolic Tradition, 16:9-11, accessed at http://www.bombaxo.com/hippolytus.html. It is intriguing to reflect on contemporary debates regarding extending church membership to same sex couples and imagine similar discussions surrounding the acceptance of Christian soldiers into the fellowship of believers. Canon 12 of the Council of Nicæa seems to make a similar point, though some scholars have suggested a censure less broad than one against military service in general is in view:
"As many as were called by grace, and displayed the first zeal, having cast aside their military girdles, but afterwards returned, like dogs, to their own vomit, (so that some spent money and by means of gifts regained their military stations); let these, after they have passed the space of three years as hearers, be for ten years prostrators" (accessed at http://www.newadvent.org/fathers/3801.htm)
60 Douglas John Hall, The Cross in Our Context: Jesus and the Suffering World, Minneapolis: Fortress Press, 2003. p. 166.

FIGHT THE POWERS

It must be admitted that there is something of an argument from silence against seeing the separationist approach as normative since the writers of the New Testament and the early church fathers wrote from a position of powerlessness.

Should it be a surprise that the leaders of an oppressed community with no recourse to the voting booth would exhort their followers to "turn the other cheek" (Matthew 5:39) when soldiers attacked them and to pray for those in authority to not molest them, so "that [they] may live peaceful and quiet lives" (1 Timothy 2:2)?

Certainly not, but as we have shown throughout this work, there is more to be said for a Christian doctrine of the separation of church and state than this. In light of the material we have surveyed as to the relationship of the demonic to the state alone, not to mention Jesus' own words regarding His non-violent kingdom, the merit of the early church/Anabaptist approach is clear.

Christendom Models

Once the church was given a privileged position by the state, beginning with the conversion of Constantine the Great in 312 A.D., it had to reconcile this newfound position of privilege with its previous stance on separation. Broadly speaking, this reconciliation was done by positing two spheres or kingdoms—one spiritual and one earthly—which crossed into each other and had to be synthesized in some fashion.

A key distinction in Roman Catholic thought was expounded in Pope Boniface VIII's 1302 papal bull Unam Sanctum, which saw one kingdom but "two swords"—one spiritual and the other temporal. The latter, wielded by the state, was of a lower order, however, giving the church a wider influence over the state than the state had over the church. This bull served the personal interests of a pope in conflict with French king Philip the Fair and argued that "outside of the Church" whose head is the pope, "there is no salvation," so the king had better temper his arrogance.

Such an approach stands in contrast to the Eastern Orthodox churches which were in practice widely under the authority of the emperor (a system referred to as caesaropapism),

Reformation models (with the exception of the radical reformation of the Anabaptists) differed in some ways from these medieval approaches, but not drastically. The Lutheran Two Kingdoms approach separated the authorities of church and state into differing realms so that they should not generally impinge upon one another. However, Luther's approach to this topic often led to a kind of spiritual schizophrenia wherein an executioner or soldier could nevertheless be a Christian performing a divine office.

So even though he "slay and stab, rob and burn, as one does to his enemy," and even though, "[he has] the teaching of Christ that they should not resist evil but endure everything" because "their government is a spiritual government, and according to the spirit they are subject to no one but Christ":

"… As to their bodies and property they are subject to the civil authority, and bound to be obedient. If then they are summoned by the civil authority to combat, they are to fight and must fight from obedience, not as Christians but as members of the whole and as obedient subjects according to the body and temporal goods. Therefore when they fight they do not do it for themselves, nor on their own account, but in the service and under the orders of the authorities under whom they are placed."[61]

The reformed model, finding expression in John Calvin and those who followed him, has sought to integrate church and state in such a way that the effect is that the distinction between them is

---

61 Martin Luther, Can Soldiers Be Christians?, accessed at
http://opensiuc.lib.siu.edu/cgi/viewcontent.cgi?article=1082&context=ocj

not always clear. Government must abide by God's law, the church must remind government of this law, and the government must enforce morality at the point of the sword. It is no wonder, then, that the modern theonomy movement has emerged primarily in reformed circles. As R.J. Rushdoony wrote in his *Christianity and the State*, even as he rails against political authoritarianism:

> "the Christian community must assert the priority of God's law-word as binding on all of life, including church, state, and school. Christians must once again take over government in education, welfare, health, and other spheres."[62]

Another view that fits broadly within the Christendom framework but still manages to distinguish itself from it is the "prophetic" model of the black church in America. It is at once among the Christendom approaches in that it seeks to enact the values of the church into policy, while at the same time distinct from them as an outsider position of oppressed people demanding justice from those in power. One may find support for this approach in Paul's demand for respect from the Roman authorities who had violated his rights (see Acts chapters 16, 22, and 23), or perhaps to Walter Wink's interpretation of the non-resistance sections of the Sermon on the Mount as the oppressed person's only means of confronting oppressive power.[63]

---

62 R.J. Rushdoony, Christianity and the State, Chalcedon/Ross House Books, 2015, Kindle edition.

63 For example, in reference to Jesus exhorting those who are sued for their shirt to give over their coat as well (Mt 5:40-42), Wink argues: "Why then does Jesus counsel them to give over their inner garment as well? This would mean stripping off all their clothing and marching out of court stark naked! Put yourself in the debtor's place, and imagine the chuckles this saying must have evoked. There stands the creditor, beet-red with embarrassment, your outer garment in one hand, your underwear in the other. You have suddenly turned the tables on him. You had no hope of winning the trial; the law was entirely in his favor. But you have refused to be humiliated, and at the same time you have registered a stunning protest against a system that spawns such debt. You have said in effect, 'You want my robe? Here, take everything! Now you've got all I have except my body. Is that what you'll take next'" (Walter Wink, Jesus and Nonviolence:

CODY COOK

A Biblical Model for Engagement

Though the conservative Anabaptist position of complete separation has much to commend it in the biblical text, there are suggestions in scripture that a more nuanced approach could be warranted. For those who are not persuaded of the strict separationist argument, some guidelines for appropriate involvement can be shaped in line with the biblical study we have undertaken in the previous section.

In short, here are the biblical emphases and counter-emphases which should act as guardrails for developing a Christian model for engaging political power:
1. The state serves a divine purpose, and yet it is also under the temporary authority of Satan—a reality which will not be finally undone until the return of Christ. There can therefore be no Christian nation this side of the parousia.

2. There are functions which the state performs which Christ commands that Christians not participate in, yet Paul could still demand that those in power meet their obligations to promote justice. We might also add an argument from silence here: though the New Testament takes a dim view of political power and forbids Christians the exercise of some of its functions, it does not explicitly forbid us from involvement in *all* of its functions. This suggests that it is at least possible for obedient Christians to participate in politics on some level.

In light of these data, a biblical philosophy for political involvement begins to emerge. Its edges are not sharply defined, but are admittedly fuzzy. It entails a church which is loyal to the kingdom of God primarily and loyal to their nation of birth only insofar as their conscience, informed by scripture, will allow them to be. Biblical Christians are good citizens primarily because they are good neighbors, showing kindness both to friend and enemy without regard to race or national origin.

Though living under a New Testament reality fundamentally different in many regards from the old covenant system, perhaps we can look to the Old Testament prophet Daniel as something of a model for what it looks like to be a citizen of one kingdom under God while simultaneously seeking to be civically minded in the pagan nation where we find ourselves in exile.

Daniel was a Judahite taken to Babylon in exile as a young man and placed into service for the empire. His integrity and hard work gained him notice, to the point that King Darius had planned to "set him over the whole kingdom" (Daniel 6:3, ESV).

This made his fellow bureaucrats jealous, so they went about looking to discredit him. They could not do so on the basis of Daniel's ethics or competency, so they settled on this scheme:
> "We shall not find any ground for complaint against this Daniel unless we find it in connection with the law of his God" (Daniel 6:5, ESV).

Realizing that Daniel's faith would not allow him to compromise his unique commitment to God by participating in the cult of the state, these officials convinced Darius to decree that if anyone made petition to any god or man besides Darius for thirty days, they would be thrown into the lion's den.

Once Daniel learned of this, he immediately went before an open window of his apartment, faced Jerusalem (a hint of the cosmic geography suggested in Deuteronomy 32:8 where God's unique authority and presence is associated with a particular location), and prayed to God.

What was Daniel's example? He served the pagan nation he was brought to with integrity and distinction, but he never forgot that he was a citizen in exile from another kingdom; nor did he allow the appeal of pragmatism or privilege to seduce him from his obligations to the one true God.

If we are, as all of Judah was in Babylon, citizens of one kingdom in exile in another, then perhaps we would also do well to follow the instructions which God gave to them:
> "But seek the welfare of the city where I have sent you into exile, and pray to the LORD on its behalf, for in its welfare you will find your welfare" (Jeremiah 29:7, ESV).

An Application of the Biblical Model

What does seeking the welfare of the city in which we are in exile look like? For one, it looks like the minimizing of violence and force so that people may freely speak, worship, and interact with each other—freedoms necessary for the church to meet and evangelize but also for commerce (the basis of survival) and the self-determination of other groups and individuals, whether that self-determination leads to their acceptance of the gospel or their rejection of it. In other words, a Christian can petition the state for the recognition of her equality and the equality of religious and ethnic minorities, as both Paul and the prophetic tradition of the black church did. Perhaps it is also not inappropriate for Christians to use protest and the voting booth (where it is available to them) to influence the state to do its duty of protecting the weak, ensuring justice, and not falling prey to corruption or the hypnotizing drum beat of war.

After all, if we are encouraged by Paul *to pray* that our leaders support human freedom instead of choosing the path of immoral interference and oppression (1 Timothy 2:2), why not also encourage the state to do so by direct action? The state may have spiritual forces behind it but it is, after all, still administered by men and women made in God's image who can be influenced by the persuasion of other human beings.

FIGHT THE POWERS

At the same time, if we are to take seriously the biblical notion of the separation of God's kingdom from the kingdoms of men, there are attitudes and approaches which are not appropriate for Christians to have when it comes to our political involvement.

One such attitude would be the desire to force others, through law, to follow our unique moral and doxological imperatives as Christians. So, for example, we should not seek to create laws which punish those in same sex sexual relationships or censure Muslims and atheists. Paul is clear that it is not our job to judge those outside of the church, but that we must leave that work to God (1 Corinthians 5:12). Because "our struggle is not against flesh and blood" (Ephesians 6:12), we should pursue the goal of transforming hearts and minds, not coercing bodies. If we are more interested in fighting culture wars than spiritual ones, we will alienate the very people we are tasked with reaching for the gospel. Instead of trying to privilege ourselves by stepping on others, we should follow the model provided by Christ, who "came not to be served but to serve" (Matthew 20:28, ESV). A Christian politics, therefore, will be a politics of service for others.

Another forbidden attitude for Christians would be one of militaristic nationalism. Jesus makes it clear that the Christian is one who turns the other cheek when he is struck (Matthew 5:39) and is loyal to a spiritual kingdom that takes precedent over the violent kingdoms of earth (John 18:36, Philippians 3:20). This extends to areas where violence is more subtle as well. For instance, a loyal subject of the kingdom of God who is also a privileged citizen of their country of residence will look at the immigrant as their sister and not seek to oppress or deprivilege her on the basis of secondary loyalties to nation or man-made laws.

Finally, the Christian cannot view the state as her messiah or lord. That position has already been filled. Freedom of worship can be a boon to the church (though a privileged status can often be a bane), but even in persecution the gates of hell will not prevail against it. Whether or not we have political influence, our obligations remain the same:

"Learn to do right; seek justice. Defend the oppressed. Take up the cause of the fatherless; plead the case of the widow" (Isaiah 1:17, NIV).

In sum, the lens through which the Christian ought to view the world should be Christ—particularly His chosen weakness in order that He might love and serve others (Philippians 2:6-9). This tactic might seem weak or foolish when looked at from the perspective of worldly wisdom, but, "the foolishness of God is wiser than men, and the weakness of God is stronger than men" (1 Corinthians 1:25, ESV). It was this weakness, after all, which defeated the powers and principalities and conquered the Roman Empire.

Such a lens requires that we repent of our desire to treat the political arena as a battleground where we wage crusades using the pagan tools of force and power to subjugate our enemies. Love demands that we go out of our way to respect the dignity of others and ensure their peace and liberty, which will in turn make them more open to defecting to God's kingdom. If we are to call everyone to the marriage supper of the lamb, we must first make room at the earthly table where we presently dine.

FIGHT THE POWERS

Conclusion

A Summary of Our Findings

The results of this study can be summarized under five major headings:

1. The Old Testament speaks univocally about the notion of patron angels over nations. It is also clear that these angels have been corrupted. Meanwhile, Israel is presented as God's special people.

2. The New Testament builds upon this theme (with a little help from Jewish intertestamental literature) but recontextualizes it in light of the coming of Christ. Christ's ministry, death, and resurrection constitute a major defeat for the "powers" and brings about a new kingdom disconnected from the methods and negative spiritual entanglements of human nations. The church, and not an earthly nation, are now God's special people.

3. This defeat of the powers is not yet fully complete. We look forward to the return of Christ to fully reclaim the nations from the powers and manifest His spiritual kingdom as a visible reality.

4. Until that happens, Christians must be wary of compromising their loyalties to the kingdom of God by becoming deeply entangled with the kingdoms of men. As Paul said in in 1 Corinthians 10:21, "you cannot drink the cup of the Lord and the cup of demons. You cannot

partake of the table of the Lord and the table of demons"
(ESV).

5. Our obligation, therefore, is to find balance: to seek to
be good citizens in a system overseen by Satan without
undermining our unique allegiance to the kingdom of God
or taking up the weapons of pagans which have been
forbidden to us.

These conclusions are in fundamental opposition to the way that
many Christians, particularly in the United States, have been
encouraged to think about the relationship between faith and
country. In the final analysis, no country can be a Christian
nation; even if some of its leaders have been influenced by good
Christian ideals such as the dignity and equality of all people or
the necessity that those in authority judge fairly to avoid
persecuting the under-privileged or giving undue consideration to
the privileged.

America may have certain Christian principles enshrined in its
founding, but the influence of the demonic (for example in our
history of racism, nativism, eugenics, and abortion) is also both
apparent and unshakable this side of Christ's return.

In other words, are weapons are not carnal, but spiritual. In our
study, we have seen that certain forms of activism and political
engagement are not inappropriate for Christians. However, just
because a Christian may involve himself in politics doesn't mean
that this is a primary means for fighting the powers and
principalities.

How to Fight the Powers

If we should not now be seeking to establish Christian rule over
the state, how should we understand God's reclaiming of the
nations at Pentecost?

Recall what we read in Genesis—that man was meant to have dominion over the world but lost that dominion to Satan, and the fallen angelic sons of God. Christ took that authority back by bringing the Kingdom of God into the world, as expressed most dramatically at Pentecost's reversal of Babel.

So we have a conundrum. Christ has defeated the powers, but he has not yet conquered world politics through His church. This tension is perhaps best expressed by the author of the epistle to the Hebrews:

> *"For it was not to angels that God subjected the world to come, of which we are speaking. It has been testified somewhere, 'What is man, that you are mindful of him, or the son of man, that you care for him? You made him for a little while lower than the angels; you have crowned him with glory and honor, putting everything in subjection under his feet.'*

> *"Now in putting everything in subjection to him, he left nothing outside his control. At present, we do not yet see everything in subjection to him. But we see him who for a little while was made lower than the angels, namely Jesus, crowned with glory and honor because of the suffering of death, so that by the grace of God he might taste death for everyone" (Hebrews 2:5-9, ESV).*

Indeed, we see Christ having conquered death and the powers through the cross and this being proclaimed to the nations, but we do not yet see the world in subjection to Him.

That's because God began to reclaim the nations not by encouraging His people to form their own government or even to vote for the candidates of his favorite political party, but simply by preaching the gospel and living out the gospel reality in how we treat others regardless of their race or nationality. God is not interested in co-opting fallen human systems of government which pervert the faith and serve the demons by dividing mankind, but in bringing people of every tribe, tongue, country, and race to defect to His kingdom.

When the crowd at Pentecost asked what they should do in light of Christ's victory, Peter did not tell them to form a Moral Majority or a Christian Coalition, but:
> "Repent and be baptized every one of you in the name of Jesus Christ for the forgiveness of your sins, and you will receive the gift of the Holy Spirit. For the promise is for you and for your children and for all who are far off, everyone whom the Lord our God calls to himself" (Acts 2:38-39, ESV).

This is the warfare we have been called to—proclaiming Christ crucified as the means of the world powers' defeat.

But that isn't the end of the matter. When Christ does return again to claim the nations, we will reign with Him in our capacity as the restored image of God. Though for now the dragon reigns as usurper over the nations, the angels who surround the throne of God have declared:
> *"Worthy are you to take the scroll and to open its seals, for you were slain, and by your blood you ransomed people for God from every tribe and language and people and nation, and you have made them a kingdom and priests to our God, and they shall reign on the earth"* *(Revelation 5:9-10, ESV).*

Suggestions for Further Reading

On Demonology, Spiritual Worldview

Arnold, C. E. (1998). *Powers of darkness: Principalities & powers in Pauls letters*. Downers Grove, IL: InterVarsity Press.

Dickason, C. F. (1995). *Angels elect and evil*. Chicago: Moody.

Heiser, M. S. (2015). *The unseen realm: Recovering the supernatural worldview of the Bible*. Bellingham, WA: Lexham Press.

Russell, D. S. (1984). *The method & message of Jewish Apocalyptic: 200BC-AD100*. Philadelphia: Westminister. Toorn, K. V.,

Becking, B., & Horst, P. W. (1999). *Dictionary of deities and demons in the Bible*. Leiden: Brill.

Unger, M. F. (2011). *Biblical demonology: A study of spiritual forces behind the present world unrest*. Kregel.

Wink, W. (2001). *Naming the powers: The language of power in the New Testament*. Minneapolis, MN: Fortress Pr.

On Politics, Church and State Issues

Benestad, J. B. (2015). *Five views on the church and politics*. Grand Rapids, MI: Zondervan.

Boyd, G. A. (2009). *The myth of a Christian nation: How the quest for political power is destroying the church*. Grand Rapids, MI: Zondervan.

Hall, D. J. (2003). *The cross in our context: Jesus and the suffering world*. Minneapolis: Fortress Press.

Kling, A. S. (2017). *The three languages of politics: Talking across the political divides*. Washington, D.C.: Cato Institute.

Levin, Y. (2014). *The great debate: Edmund Burke, Thomas Paine, and the birth of right and left*. New York: Basic Books.

Niebuhr, H. R. (2003). *Christ & culture*. New York: HarperCollins World.

Sprinkle, P. M. (2013). *Fight: A Christian case for nonviolence*. Colorado Springs, CO: David C Cook.

Tertullian, *De corona militis*

Williams, D.K. (2012) *God's own party: the making of the Christian right*. New York: Oxford University Press.

Wink, W. (2003). *Jesus and nonviolence: A third way*. Minneapolis, MN: Fortress.

About the Author

Cody Cook is a theology graduate student and film buff living in Cincinnati, Ohio with his wife Raven, daughter Ava, and cat Jobyna.

His other books, articles, and podcast can be found at www.cantus-firmus.com

Other works by Cody Cook available on Kindle and at www.cantus-firmus.com:

A Second Adam
(also in paperback)

Post- Enlightened
(also in paperback)

Open Source Jesus

Made in the USA
Las Vegas, NV
10 September 2024